THE ULTIMATE GUIDE TO
EASY PLANT-BASED COOKING FOR ONE (OR TWO)

Nourishing Anti-Inflammatory Recipes

Michelle De La Mora

Skyhorse Publishing

Copyright © 2025 by Michelle De La Mora
All photos by Shutterstock and Michelle De La Mora, except for portrait photos taken by Joshua Flint

All rights reserved. No part of this book may be reproduced in any manner without the express written consent of the publisher, except in the case of brief excerpts in critical reviews or articles. All inquiries should be addressed to Skyhorse Publishing, 307 West 36th Street, 11th Floor, New York, NY 10018.

Skyhorse Publishing books may be purchased in bulk at special discounts for sales promotion, corporate gifts, fund-raising, or educational purposes. Special editions can also be created to specifications. For details, contact the Special Sales Department, Skyhorse Publishing, 307 West 36th Street, 11th Floor, New York, NY 10018 or info@skyhorsepublishing.com.

Skyhorse® and Skyhorse Publishing® are registered trademarks of Skyhorse Publishing, Inc.®, a Delaware corporation.

Visit our website at www.skyhorsepublishing.com.

10 9 8 7 6 5 4 3 2 1

Library of Congress Cataloging-in-Publication Data is available on file.

Cover design by Kai Texel
Cover photo courtesy of Shutterstock.com

Print ISBN: 978-1-5107-8265-5
Ebook ISBN: 978-1-5107-8266-2

Printed in China

To make the recipe pictured on the front cover, see Pasta alla Bella Capri on page 195.

The information and recipes provided in this cookbook are for educational purposes only and are not intended as medical advice. While the content is aimed at supporting an anti-inflammatory lifestyle, individual reactions to ingredients can vary. Those with inflammatory conditions such as Crohn's disease, GERD, IBS, and other medical issues should consult with a healthcare professional before making dietary changes. The advice and strategies offered here may not be suitable for everyone. The author and publisher are not responsible for any adverse effects that may result from the using this cookbook.

To Arthur Theodore, my precious one,
In your tiny hands, the world's begun.
At just three years, you bring such light,
Your joy in the kitchen makes everything right.

We mix and stir with laughter so sweet,
Creating memories that feel complete.
Your eyes sparkle with each dish we make,
A bond so strong that time can't shake.

This book is yours, a treasure from me,
A token of love for you to see.
May you always find wonder in the flavors you explore,
And know you've made my heart forever soar.

Also by Michelle De La Mora, formerly known as Michelle Savage...

The Green Aisle's Smoothies & Slushies
The Green Aisle's Healthy Indulgence
The Green Aisle's Healthy Juicing
The Ultimate Guide to Healthy juicing

Contents

The Ultimate Guide to Easy Plant-Based Cooking 1
Hello, Wonderful Readers! 3
Background 6
Healthy Cooking Hacks 9
Exploring Plant-Based Counterparts 16
Recommended Plant-Based Brands Featured in This Cookbook......19
Considerations for Disease or Illness 26
Mind & Body Nutrition 34
The Importance of an Anti-Inflammatory Diet 40

RECIPES

The Beverage Oasis 45
The Art of Breakfast 69
Nibble Bliss 89
Simmering Soup 107
Midday Munchies Unleashed 123
Elevated Evening Soiree 155
Sweet Indulgence 203
Special Artisan Creations 231
Occasional Indulgences 245

Understanding Sugar & Glycemic Index (GI)..................................259
Contributors..264
Resources...271
Acknowledgments..273
Metric Conversions..274
Index...275

The Ultimate Guide to Easy Plant-Based Cooking

Anti-inflammatory Recipes for One (Or Two)

Are you tired of the same old meals and craving exciting flavors to reignite your passion for healthy eating? Look no further! *The Ultimate Guide to Easy Plant-Based Cooking* is your essential companion, designed to inspire delicious, plant-based meals perfect for solo dining or a cozy dinner for two.

Building on the success of the award-winning *Ultimate Guide for Healthy Juicing*, which proudly received the Bronze Award from the Living Now Book Awards, this collection offers a diverse array of vibrant and savory dishes. Whether you're transitioning from an intermittent detox juice cleanse, maintaining a health-conscious lifestyle, or seeking the simplest way to prepare nutritious meals without falling into the yo-yo diet trap, these recipes offer a range of irresistible options to bring excitement back to your kitchen.

Emphasizing clean eating as the cornerstone of lasting health, each recipe supports your journey into the world of plant-based nutrition. Celebrating the power of whole, natural ingredients, these dishes deliver balanced flavors, textures, and nutrients, making healthy eating both delicious and enjoyable.

But there's more to this cookbook than just recipes. It's a holistic guide to wellness through mindful eating. In the following pages, we'll delve into the principles of anti-inflammatory nutrition, gut health optimization, strategies for overall vitality, proper absorption, recognizing food as medicine, and mindful eating practices. Alongside these delicious recipes, you'll find a lightbulb icon to spark your creativity. This icon invites you to unleash your inner chef by experimenting with flavor pairing, ingredient substitution, and improvisation, transforming each recipe into a personalized masterpiece.

Before delving into the recipes, let's explore how this cookbook can revolutionize your approach to plant-based cooking. Immerse yourself in a collection of recipes crafted for various levels of expertise, from the effortless "Weeknight Wonders" (One Spoon) to the more ambitious "Weekend Showstoppers" (Three Spoons). Whether you're a seasoned cook or a novice, each recipe is accompanied by a helpful rating indicating its level of simplicity. This provides you with the choice to select recipes suited to your comfort level, making cooking an enjoyable and gratifying experience. As you conquer the recipes rated with one spoon, progress to those with three spoons, thus embracing the opportunity to elevate your cooking skills and explore new horizons.

Get ready for a unique cooking experience with this trusted companion. Venture into a world of vibrant spices, new ingredients, and mouthwatering plant-based creations. Revitalize your meals while nurturing your body, and relish the amazing flavors of a plant-centered lifestyle. Start your journey today and discover how easy it is to make not only healthy but truly delicious meals!

Hello, Wonderful Readers!

My name is Michelle De La Mora, formerly known as Michelle Savage, and I'm excited to welcome you to my world of flavors and foodie adventures. From the sun-kissed beaches of California to the rolling hills and breathtaking vistas of Jasper Highlands, Tennessee—where I now reside as a newlywed—my culinary journey has taken me on a whirlwind tour of tastes, textures, and experiences. And I'm now thrilled to invite you into my kitchen to share in the joy and wonder of easy, delicious plant-based cooking.

As an Amen Clinics Brain Health Professional and Institute for Integrative Nutrition Health Coach, my career has been dedicated to promoting healthy eating and lifestyle changes. This cookbook is more than just a collection of recipes; it's a reflection of everything I'm passionate about. It's about celebrating the beauty of nature's bounty, embracing the simplicity of whole foods, and finding joy in every moment spent whipping up something tasty. Even more important, it's about enjoying calories, not counting them, because life is too short not to savor every bite.

Have you ever stopped to think about why cooking holds such a special place in our hearts?

Sure, we all need to eat, but isn't it amazing how food creates moments of pure joy and connection around the table? Nothing beats the feeling of sharing a delicious homemade meal with loved ones. Whether it's cozying up with your partner and kids, catching up with your folks, or laughing over last week's adventure with your besties, the moments become even more special over a beautifully prepared dinner.

And cooking? It's like a love letter you can taste. It's a way of saying to your favorite people, "You mean the world to me."

To each and every one of you who has picked up this book, I say thank you. Thank you for your curiosity, your open-mindedness, and your willingness to explore new flavors and ideas.

Together, let's savor the goodness of life, one delicious recipe at a time.

As you dive into these pages, I encourage you to experiment, make these recipes your own, and share your culinary creations with those you love. Let's create beautiful memories and delicious meals together.

Here's to a Happy & Healthy YOU,

Michelle De La Mora

Background

Michelle De La Mora AKA Savage (b. 1970)

Amen Clinics Brain Health Professional & Institute for Integrative Nutrition Health Coach.

Michelle De La Mora, formerly known as Michelle Savage, is a dynamic figure in the field of holistic health and wellness. With a lifelong passion for promoting healthy eating and lifestyle changes, she is the esteemed author of the Green Aisle Series, a collection of game-changing books that make healthy living both fun and accessible. Her acclaimed works include *The Green Aisle's Healthy Smoothies & Slushies*, *The Green Aisle's Healthy Indulgence*, *The Green Aisle's Healthy Juicing*, and *The Ultimate Guide to Healthy Juicing*.

Qualifications

- Amen Clinics Certified Brain Health Professional
- Certified Integrative Nutrition Health Coach with specialized training in gut health

Training and Education

Michelle received her professional training and certification from Amen University under the mentorship of Dr. Daniel G. Amen and the Institute for Integrative Nutrition in New York City, guided by Joshua Rosenthal, Founder and Director for INHC.

Accomplishments

Michelle's dedication to health and wellness has garnered widespread recognition, including:

- **Living Now Book Award (Bronze):** *The Green Aisle's Healthy Juicing* was honored with the prestigious Bronze Award for its exceptional contribution to enhancing the quality of life through healthy living.

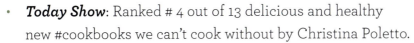

- **Formal Congratulations:** Received commendation from Representative Jeff Denham of the US Congress for contributions to improving the region's health.
- *Today Show*: Ranked # 4 out of 13 delicious and healthy new #cookbooks we can't cook without by Christina Poletto.
- *Good Day Sacramento*: Featuring a vibrant appearance showcasing *The Green Aisle's Healthy Smoothies & Slushies*, the segment brought a burst of flavor to viewers' screens with an impromptu creation of the Strawberry Cheesecake Smoothie.
- *Manteca Bulletin:* Featured article highlighting Michelle's efforts to promote health in the community.
- **Great Valley Bookfest**: Conducted presentations, healthy cooking demos, and engaged in free gift and raffle giveaways.
- **Barnes & Noble Book Signing**: Hosted a successful "New Year, New You" event in Modesto, California, featuring book signings and discussions.
- **Rose & Remmington Book Signing Event**: Michelle hosted a successful book signing event at Rose & Remmington in Hamilton Place, Chattanooga, Tennessee, showcasing cookbook recipes alongside Green Aisle signature mugs and bowls. Guests enjoyed exclusive in-store discounts.

Publications, Reviews & Media
- Skyhorse Publishing
- Living Now Book Award (Bronze)
- *Today Show*
- Barnes & Noble
- *Good Day Sacramento*
- Great Valley Bookfest

- *Writers & Authors on Fire* by John Vonhof (Podcast Appearance)
- Christian Books: Top eBooks in Health & Fitness
- Cookbooks 365
- Fit Life Pursuits
- *Publishers Weekly*
- Chefs Cook at Home

Visit GreenAisleWellness.com to explore Michelle De La Mora's comprehensive biography, connect through fan mail, and find links to purchase her healthy cookbooks and educational eBooks. Discover how she empowers wellness as the CEO and founder of Green Aisle Wellness.

Healthy Cooking Hacks

Elevate Your Culinary Game
Oil-Free Cooking
Inflammation can often be exacerbated by certain cooking methods, particularly when low smoke point oils are used for browning or sautéing. *But fear not!* There are alternatives that not only promote health but also enhance the flavors of your dishes. One such method is to utilize water or broth for cooking vegetables, eliminating the need for oil while still achieving delicious results. For further insights into making informed choices for health when it comes to cooking oils, be sure to check out the infographic and chapter titled "Decoding Cooking Oils" on page 13.

Budget-Friendly Blueberries
I stumbled upon a wallet-friendly trick while experimenting with ingredients for this cookbook: frozen organic blueberries. Upon defrosting them, I discovered a pool of sweet juices at the bottom of the bowl. These juices are a delicious addition to yogurt bowls, pancakes, and numerous other dishes, providing a burst of flavor without added sugars or syrups.

Homemade Vegetable Broth
Say goodbye to store-bought vegetable broth and hello to homemade goodness! Start by collecting a variety of vegetable scraps, such as carrot tops, onion skins, celery fronds, and mushroom stems. Store them in the freezer until you've gathered enough to fill a large pot three-quarters full. Cover the scraps with water and add a pinch of sea

salt and pepper and your favorite herbs and spices. Let it simmer for a couple of hours, then strain the liquid, allowing it to cool before transferring it to mason jars. This eco-friendly method not only reduces waste but also yields a delicious, nutrient-rich base for your recipes.

Mindful Seasoning

Be mindful of the quality of your seasonings. Opt for nonirradiated herbs and spices, as irradiation—a process that uses ionizing radiation to eliminate bacteria and pests—can reduce their nutritional value and potency. Additionally, avoid oversalting or over-seasoning your food, as it can mask the natural flavors of your ingredients and lead to unnecessary sodium intake.

Time-Saving Techniques

Efficiency is key in the kitchen. Before diving into a recipe, thoroughly review both the ingredients and directions, and plan out your preparation accordingly. This not only includes chopping and gathering all ingredients but also laying them out for quick access when you need them. Prepping ingredients beforehand can streamline the cooking process and ensure timely execution, especially in some recipes where timing is crucial. Additionally, this proactive approach allows you to confidently incorporate any suggested author's notes, substitution ideas, or tips into your cooking routine.

Flavor Balancing

Achieving a harmonious balance of flavors is essential in plant-based cooking. Pay close attention to the full recipe description, as it often includes substitution ideas and tips for adjusting seasonings to suit your taste preference.

Author's Notes

Keep an eye out for asterisks (*) next to certain ingredients, as they indicate *Author's Notes* regarding dietary preferences or alternative options. These notes are designed to help you customize recipes to align with your specific needs and preferences.

Cooking Tools I Can't Live Without!
Indispensable Kitchen Companions!

While some may have a passion for fashion or gadgets, mine lies in the kitchen with essential tools. These items are indispensable, enabling the creation of delicious meals every day. While quality equipment is important, I understand that not everyone can invest in them.

Below is a list of the tools I personally use in my kitchen, along with the versatile recipes they help create. However, there are many budget-friendly alternatives for each item. Remember, the key isn't the brand or model, but having the right tool to elevate your cooking experience. So whether you're a novice cook or a seasoned chef, there's always a solution to make it work within your means.

Blendtec High-Speed Blender with Twister Jar Attachment: A powerful and priceless kitchen essential for that restaurant-style smoothie like the Berry Burst Smoothie and Raspberry & Cardamom Smoothie. It's also indispensable for making homemade desserts such as Rocky Road Fudge, Luxurious Chocolate Masterpieces, and Salted Caramel Fondue.

Ceramic Dutch Oven for Bread: A must-have tool for baking loaves, such as the Dutch Oven Cheesy Jalapeño Artisan Bread. This ensures even heat distribution for a perfect outer crust and a soft, chewy center. It's also great for making Spicy Aztec Soup.

Flexible Serrated Paring Knife: Versatile and precise, ideal for trimming lemon peels and creating smooth slices.

Food Processor: A versatile tool for chopping ingredients quickly and making recipes such as the Maple Almond Chocolate Chip Oat Cookie Dough, Coconut Date Energy Bites, Chimichurri Chickpea & Avocado Sandwich, and Nutty Parmesan.

Immersion Blender: A must-have for blending soups and sauces directly in the pot, achieving smooth and creamy texture. Easily blend to your preferred consistency, whether chunky or smooth. Perfect for recipes like Pear Jam and Garlic Mashed Potatoes & Sweet Corn.

Julienne Handheld Peeler: Handy for creating thin strips and removing outer layers of vegetables, as well as adding visual appeal to dishes. Ideal for preparing the Zen Garden Salad with Sesame-Lime Dressing or adding julienned carrots to your Citrus Crunch Mac, a variation of the Chilled Tofu Mac Salad recipe.

Quick Heat Measuring Gauge: Essential for precise temperature control in liquids and hot oil, ensuring accurate cooking results. Crucial for preparing yeasts for Dutch Oven Cheesy Jalapeño Artisan Bread and Neapolitan-Style Pizza crust, and achieving the ideal temperature for Abuela's Fried Sopes.

9-Quart Cast-Iron Dutch Oven for Sopes: A robust choice for Abuela's Fried Sopes, ensuring consistent, high-quality results every time.

Ramekins: Perfect for serving individual portions and elevating the presentation of your Cheesy Jalapeño Pop'n Breakfast Cups.

Large Serrated Bread Knife: Slice with ease to avoid squashing the soft interior of your beautifully crafted Dutch Oven Cheesy Jalapeño Artisan Bread.

Silicone Molds: Ideal for creating custom-shaped Luxurious Chocolate Masterpieces, and adding a personal touch to your sweet creations. These molds offer quick release and are oven safe, making them perfect for various baking projects. They can be used for recipes such as Maple Almond Chocolate Chip Oat Cookie Dough Pops, Rocky Road Fudge, Fun Orange Treats, Salted Caramel Chews, and Strawberry Fields Forever Donuts.

Toaster Oven: Efficient for toasting, baking, and roasting smaller portions, saving time and energy. This versatile appliance is frequently used throughout this cookbook, which is designed for recipes for one or two people. Some of the delicious recipes you can make with a toaster oven include Cheesy Jalapeño Pop'n Breakfast Cups, Popcorn Paradise with sizzling Vegan Pepperoni, roasted garlic for Garlic Mashed Potatoes & Sweet Corn, Golden Spice Puff Pockets, Maple-Smoked Plant Ribbons, and Neapolitan-Style Pizza.

Having the right tools at your disposal will aid in efficiency, precision, and the overall cooking experience, allowing you to explore your culinary creativity with confidence and achieve perfect dishes every time.

Decoding Cooking Oils
Making Informed Choices for Health

Understanding the impact of cooking oils is essential in our quest for better health. Heating oils beyond their smoke point can release harmful compounds, negatively impacting both flavor and quality. Refer to the accompanying infographic for a clear breakdown of oil smoke points and their significance, providing valuable insights for making informed kitchen decisions.

Throughout the cookbook, feel free to explore and experiment with various oils to find what suits you. While specific oils, such as avocado or coconut oil, may be suggested in recipes, it's important to listen to your body and adjust as necessary. If you're sensitive to oils with high smoke points, consider using water or broth as alternatives. Just note that you may need to continue adding the liquid a little at a time while sautéing to maintain moisture and flavor. Trust your instincts and tailor recipes to suit your unique preferences and requirements.

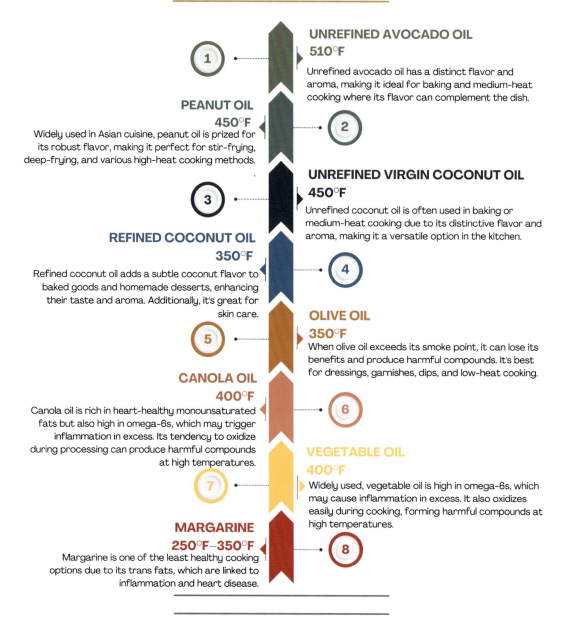

Unveiling Labels
Inflammation, Gluten, Sugar, and Grain Impacts
Reading food labels is vital for safeguarding your health. Additives and preservatives, such as aspartame, high-fructose corn syrup, and artificial colors (such as Yellow #5, Blue #1, and Red #40, just to name a few) have been linked to health issues. Understanding what goes into your food and scrutinizing ingredient choices is essential. To make informed decisions, consider using apps like Yuka, which help identify the health impact of ingredients by scanning food labels. Whenever possible, opt for whole foods and make your own meals for better control over what you consume.

Navigating the supermarket can be overwhelming, with marketing tactics everywhere. Focus on choosing fresh, organic produce, supporting local farmers, and opting for seasonal foods for the best nutrition, flavor, and value. Avoid nonorganic GMO produce to protect your health and the environment. Your grocery choices impact both your well-being and the planet.

Yuka Gem
Mastering Label Decoding
Unlock the secrets of label decoding with the Yuka app, your go-to companion for mindful and ethical cooking. This innovative tool empowers you to select clean, chemical-free ingredients effortlessly. Simply download the app, scan items in-store, and discover a wealth of information, including chemical composition and potential health impacts. With a scale ranging from 0 to 100, the higher the score, the cleaner and healthier the  product. Keep in mind that lower scores may simply indicate a higher sodium content or calorie count, which may not be harmful in moderation. It's important to interpret scores in the context of your health goals. Make informed purchasing decisions by scanning products and researching through the app, especially if you have specific dietary restrictions or health concerns.

Empower yourself to make informed, health-conscious choices as you explore the world of clean eating with Yuka!

Exploring Plant-Based Counterparts

A Flavorful Expedition

Step into this chapter dedicated to elevating your plant-based cooking experience! Discover a thoughtfully curated selection of alternative brands, ensuring flawless results with each recipe. As you navigate through these options, uncover a diverse range of plant-powered substitutions, adding a creative and delectable touch to every dish.

Whenever a recipe calls for ingredients such as butter, sour cream, eggs, meat, or cheese, you'll find their plant-based counterparts within this collection. Take the opportunity to experiment with these alternatives, enriching your kitchen repertoire with wholesome goodness.

Check out the list below for recommended plant-based brands featured in these recipes, or feel free to begin your own exploration with plant-based substitutes. While many of these products are generally healthier than their animal-based counterparts, it's important to be mindful of individual sensitivities and potential inflammatory effects.

Embrace the Spectrum of Flavors

While meat crumbles and soyrizo may not align with every dietary preference due to their higher sodium levels and processed ingredients, their inclusion offers a bridge for those transitioning to a plant-based lifestyle. By providing familiar textures and tastes, they ensure accessibility without sacrificing variety. This cookbook also includes homemade meat substitutes such as Vegan Pepperoni, Eggplant Bacon, and Barbecue Italian Beyond Loaf. Additionally, explore the cheese recipes, including Cashew Cheese Sauce, Ricotta Balls, and Tofu Feta, for more deliciously healthy plant-based options.

Your journey toward a plant-based lifestyle is as diverse as the ingredients on your plate. So, explore, experiment, and savor each flavorful step. Your kitchen is your playground, and every dish is an opportunity to celebrate the colorful world of plant-based cooking.

By making your own meat substitutes and cheeses, you can control the ingredients and ensure they are as healthy as possible. One of my favorite homemade substitutes is the Vegan Pepperoni contributed by Sarah Bond (page 250). It's perfect for adding a spicy kick to your pizzas and to the Jalapeño Pizza Crunch Melt (page 125).

Special Artisan Creations
Crafted Flavors for the Discerning Palate

Indulge in a selection of meticulously crafted recipes designed to elevate your culinary experience. This chapter includes delicious and unique creations like Cashew Cheese Sauce, Ricotta Balls, Parmesan, Tofu Feta, Eggplant Bacon, and Pickled Jalapeños & Pickles. Each recipe is tailored to bring out the best in plant-based ingredients, providing a burst of flavor in every bite. These recipes focus on anti-inflammatory ingredients, ensuring they align with a health-conscious lifestyle while delivering gourmet tastes.

Occasional Indulgences
Guilty Pleasures for Special Moments

Sometimes, a little indulgence is necessary. This chapter features recipes that, while not strictly aligned with anti-inflammatory principles, offer variety and satisfy those occasional cravings. Enjoy creations like Easy Flour Tortillas, Vegan Pepperoni, Dutch Oven Cheesy Jalapeño Artisan Bread, and Strawberry Fields Forever Donuts. These recipes are perfect for those special moments when you want to treat yourself and enjoy something truly delicious.

Plant-based substitutes not only cater to various dietary preferences but also offer numerous health benefits, including reduced inflammation and improved heart health.

Magnifying Glass Symbol

Spot the magnifying glass symbol as you browse throughout the cookbook. It's like having a friend nudging you to make sure each recipe fits just right with your dietary needs and preferences.

I'd love to hear about your culinary adventures! Share your favorite plant-based substitutions and recipes with me at Green Aisle Wellness.

Recommended Plant-Based Brands Featured in This Cookbook

Butter:
- **Miyoko's Cultured Vegan Butter, Misha's Black Truffle Cheese, or Naturli' European Style Plant Butter Spread:** Perfect for spreading and cooking, these plant-based alternatives offer a luxurious buttery taste. They provide a potentially healthier option compared to conventional butter, especially when they include beneficial oils like avocado oil.

Buffalo Sauce:
- **Primal Kitchen Avocado Oil Buffalo Sauce (8.5-ounce bottle):** Crafted from rich avocado oil and cayenne pepper, delivering a pure and delicious taste without the use of natural flavors or xanthan gum. This sauce is featured in the Blazing Buffalo Cauliflower with Blue Cheese Crumbles recipe and is a good option for those concerned with inflammation.

Cheese Crumbles:
- **Nuts For Cheese and Rebel Cheese:** Fantastic choices for plant-based cheese, made with wholesome ingredients such as organic cashews, coconut milk, and nutritional yeast, delivering a rich, savory flavor and creamy texture. Unlike many commercial brands that use additives and artificial ingredients, Rebel Cheese offers a cleaner ingredient list, focusing on whole foods and exceptional taste. These cheeses are completely dairy-free, egg-free, and honey-free. Perfect for those seeking healthy, flavorful cheese alternatives. For homemade options,

try making Cashew Cheese Sauce, Cashew Crèma Mexicana, Ricotta Balls, Parmesan, and Tofu Feta using the recipes found throughout this cookbook.

Cheese Spread:
- **Plant Perks Smoked Gouda Plant-Based Cheeze Spread:** Infuse a touch of smoky Gouda goodness into your dishes with this delectable spread. Its creamy and savory profile is used in the Fire-Kissed Gouda Bites, Blistering Shishitos with Feta, and Fiesta Smoked Crème recipes.

Cheese & Meats:
- Rebel Cheese is leading the way in the plant-based cheese industry by offering delicious and innovative alternatives to traditional dairy products. By applying the same artisanal cheesemaking techniques as the dairy industry, but to plant-based mediums, Rebel Cheese achieves those flavors and textures we all know and love. All of their cheeses are 100 percent vegan and dairy-free, handcrafted from their house-made milks and using only real ingredients like organic cashews and no preservatives or artificial flavors.
- Rebel Cheese's cheeses do not contain gluten ingredients, though they are all nut-based and some may include soy and sesame. For a full list of ingredients, allergens, and nutrition information, visit the "Meet the Cheeses" page on their website. For additional questions, reach out to cheeseclub@rebelcheese.com.
- In addition to cheeses, Rebel Cheese also offers house-made plant-based meats, and partners with local Austin companies to provide other accoutrements, like jams and crackers. Rebel Cheese's mission is to prove that vegan products can be better for ourselves, the animals, and the planet—without compromising on taste. The brand has garnered significant recognition, winning in three categories at the 2024 VegNews Cheese Awards, with more than 110,000 people voting. They were also featured on *Shark Tank* (season 15, episode 9, aired on December 15, 2023), where they showcased their groundbreaking approach to plant-based foods. Rebel Cheese also has

two brick-and-mortar locations: a bistro in Austin, Texas, and a cheese shop in New York City. Without a doubt, Rebel Cheese will become your one-stop shop for your plant-based charcuterie needs, whether you are shopping online or in person!
- Vegan cheeses are made with gluten-free ingredients but may contain traces of gluten due to shared kitchen space with gluten-based products like seitan.

"Austin-based Rebel Cheese is innovating the cheese industry by applying artisanal dairy cheesemaking techniques to plant-based mediums, crafting real cheese from plants. By achieving the textures and flavors of cheese through more sustainable means, we're reshaping the cheese paradigm to evolve the traditions we love."

—www.RebelCheese.com

Noochy Licious (Nutritional Yeast):

- Another must-have for plant-based cheese lovers is Noochy Licious, a premium nutritional yeast from Gloriously Vegan. Packed with bold,  cheesy flavor and a rich nutrient profile, Noochy Licious is perfect for adding depth to sauces, dressings, and cheesy dishes—without any dairy—and is a key ingredient in several recipes throughout this cookbook, including Creamy Caprese Seduction, Chilled Tofu Mac , Guilt-Free Cheesy Nut Mac, Garlic Mashed Potatoes & Sweet Corn, White Cheddar & Broccoli, Cashew Basil Blitz, Cashew Crème Fraîche, Cashew Crèma Mexicana, Nutty Parmesan, and Maple-Smoked Plant Ribbons.

"Founded with a passion for great taste and sustainability, Gloriously Vegan is dedicated to providing delicious, nutritious alternatives that bring joy to plant-based living. Whether you're a committed vegan or just exploring new flavors, their products make it easy to enjoy wholesome, plant-based cheese."

—GloriouslyVegan.com

Dried Cherries:

- **Unsweetened Tart Cherries by Herbalia:** These tangy dried cherries add a burst of flavor and are the perfect ingredient for the Chunky Cherry Chocolate Sorbet recipe. Tart cherries are known for their anti-inflammatory properties.

Eggs:

- **JUST Egg:** A plant-based alternative made from mung beans, offering 5 to 6 grams of protein per serving. Perfect for those with egg allergies, it's a star player in the Cheesy Jalapeño Pop'n Breakfast Cup recipe. This product is less likely to cause inflammation compared to traditional eggs.

Meat Grounds:

- **Beyond Beef Plant-Based Ground:** Ideal for the Barbecue Italian Beyond Loaf and Rustic Cornbread Skillet variation recipe used in this book, delivering a meaty texture without the meat.

Mozzarella:

- **Plant Ahead and Nuts for Cheese**: Offer cleaner ingredient lists and a melt-in-your-mouth experience. It's important to be aware that many commercial brands contain harmful additives such as calcium phosphate, cellulose, and dextrose, a starch-based sugar linked to inflammation. For those seeking a cleaner option, consider brands like Plant Ahead and Nuts for Cheese.

For homemade options, try making Ricotta Balls or the recipes found in the Special Artisan Creations chapter at the end of the book.

Pasta:
- **Banza:** Revitalize your pasta dishes by using Banza pasta options, celebrated for their increased protein and decreased carbohydrates. Not only do they offer a guilt-free and satisfying meal option, but they support gut health with prebiotics, offering benefits like inflammation reduction by nurturing beneficial gut microbes. Alternatively, you can create a fresh and healthy option by spiralizing zucchini to make zoodles. Sauté these vibrant zoodles for a light, low-carb, and nutrient-packed alternative to traditional pasta. Whether you choose Banza pasta or zoodles, both options offer a great way to enjoy your favorite pasta dishes while promoting better health.

Pepperoni
- **Field Roast Classic Pizzeria Plant-Based Pepperoni:** Perfect for the Jalapeño Pizza Crunch Melt, Carb-Free Pizza Bowl, or Neapolitan-Style Pizza recipes, this option delivers smoky and savory notes. Unlike traditional pepperoni, which can cause inflammation due to its processed nature, high salt content, synthetic nitrates, and saturated fat, Field Roast Plant-Based Pepperoni is a better alternative. However, it may still cause some inflammation due to texturizing agents, carrageenan, anticaking agents, and gluten.

For a healthier homemade alternative, try Sarah Bond's Vegan Pepperoni recipe (page 250). While it contains gluten, it uses healthier ingredients overall.

Pickle Chips:
- **Grillo's Pickle Chips**: Bursting with garlic and dill, providing a fresh crunch. For a homemade alternative, consider using the Prosecco Pickled Jalapeños recipe (page 242) and replace the jalapeños with cucumber slices. Made from natural ingredients, these pickles are a fantastic option for those following an anti-inflammatory diet.

Ramen:
- **Lotus Foods Organic Jade Pear Rice Ramen Noodles**: Highlighted in the PhoMazing Soup recipe, these gluten-free noodles offer a healthier alternative to traditional ramen. Made from rice, they tend to be gentler on the system compared to wheat-based noodles.

Seasoning:
- **Frontier Co-Op Pizza Seasoning**: Elevate the flavors of Jalapeño Pizza Crunch Melt, Carb-Free Pizza Bowl, and Neapolitan-Style Pizza recipes with this robust blend. Perfect for pizza enthusiasts, this seasoning is crafted from a blend of herbs and spices, free from MSG, artificial flavors, preservatives, and other undesirable additives, making it an excellent choice for those seeking anti-inflammatory options.

Sour Cream:
- **Forager Organic Dairy-Free Sour Cream or Treeline Cheesemakers Non-Dairy Cashew Sour Cream**: Great for topping soups or enhancing spreads and dips. These are made from plant-based ingredients and are generally less inflammatory than dairy-based sour cream.

Sun-Dried Tomato Halves with Herbs:
- **California Sun-Dried Tomatoes**: Delivering the perfect blend of sun-kissed sweetness and Mediterranean herbs infused with every bite. Featured in the recipes Fire-Kissed Gouda Bites and Creamy Caprese Seduction for a bust of richness to your dish. These are generally not inflammatory.

Sun-Dried Tomato Paste:
- **Amore Sun-Dried Tomato Paste:** Infuse a rich, concentrated flavor into your Savory Tofu Scramble on Sun-Dried Slathered Toast and Jalapeño Pizza Crunch Melt recipes. While generally not inflammatory, as it's made from

tomatoes, it does contain a high amount of sodium. If you are watching your sodium intake, consider using Amore sun-dried tomatoes (not the paste) and blend them yourself.

Tomato Sauce:

- **Rao's Arrabbiata Sauce**: This sauce brings a zesty and spicy tomato goodness to the Neapolitan-Style Pizza recipe (page 248), making it a healthy and flavorful choice. Made from high-quality tomatoes and a blend of spices, it is a great option for those seeking a robust taste. However, its spiciness might not be suitable for everyone, particularly for sensitive individuals. For a milder, homemade alternatively, consider trying Mangiameli's Family Spaghetti Sauce (page 168). This allows for a personalized touch and control over the spice level.

Enjoy the possibilities of plant-based cooking with these carefully chosen alternatives, each enhancing the palette of flavors drawn from the abundance of nature. Discover a diverse range of delicious dishes, and remember, there are countless plant-based brands to explore. Expand your culinary horizons, savor what appeals to your taste, and cultivate a repertoire of delectable plant-based creations.

Considerations for Disease or Illness

Inflammation Triggers

This section explores how certain foods can act as inflammation triggers for individuals with specific health conditions. From gluten sensitivities to inflammatory responses to various grains, understanding these triggers is crucial for managing and improving overall health. This guide provides detailed insights to help you make informed dietary choices, focusing on how these triggers affect well-being and offering strategies for navigating dietary options effectively.

Author's Note:

Not all fruits and vegetables suit everyone's health needs. If you have conditions such as diabetes, rheumatoid arthritis, autoimmune diseases, SIBO (small intestinal bacterial overgrowth), IBS, leaky gut, gout, candidiasis, hypoglycemia, or similar illnesses, it's essential to be mindful of specific foods. Here are some examples of what to watch for:

- **Candida:** Limit or avoid nutritional yeast, starchy vegetables, legumes (including peanuts and cashews), processed lunch meats, high-sugar fruits and dried fruit, grains and flours containing gluten (e.g., rice, oats), dairy (especially milk and kefir), artificial sugar substitutes (e.g., brown rice syrup, corn syrup, agave, honey, maple syrup), molasses, vinegar, refined vegetable oils, processed foods, and yeast-containing foods such as kombucha, alcohol, wine, cheese, dried fruits, and bread. These foods can promote yeast growth and worsen symptoms of candidiasis.
- **Diabetes and Hypoglycemia:** Monitor and limit high-glycemic foods that can cause blood sugar spikes such as refined sugars, high-sugar fruits, and white

foods such as white sugar, white flour, white bread, and white rice. These foods can rapidly increase blood sugar levels and should be consumed in moderation or avoided to maintain stable blood sugar levels.

- **Inflammatory Diseases (e.g., autoimmune disease, lupus, rheumatoid arthritis):** Avoid nightshades such as tomatoes, potatoes, eggplant, and peppers (cayenne, paprika, tomatillos, chili peppers, bell peppers) as they may worsen symptoms. Gluten can also trigger inflammation and exacerbate symptoms in individuals with these conditions.
- **Kidney Stones:** Limit or avoid high-oxalate vegetables such as beets, chard, spinach, potatoes, nuts, nut milks, and chocolate. These foods can contribute to the formation of kidney stones in individuals prone to this condition. Staying well-hydrated and incorporating calcium-rich foods can help prevent oxalate from binding in the kidneys, reducing the risk of stone formation. Additionally, avoid excessive sodium and animal protein, as they can increase acid levels in the blood. This condition, called acidosis, can impair kidney function and raise the risk of kidney stones.
- **SIBO and IBS:** Limit or avoid nutritional yeast and other fermentable foods that can exacerbate symptoms. *Nutritional yeast* is low FODMAP and only mildly fermentable. However, some individuals—particularly those with SIBO or IBS—may experience gas and bloating. *Raw vegetables* are difficult to digest and can cause bloating. *Starchy vegetables* such as potatoes and plantains can ferment in the gut and worsen symptoms. *Dried fruit* is high in fermentable sugars and fiber, which can exacerbate symptoms. Fructose is a fermentable sugar that can cause bloating and gas. *Gluten* can cause inflammation and exacerbate symptoms in some individuals with IBS or SIBO. *Wild rice and corn* are difficult to digest and can cause fermentation. *Beans and grains* are high in fermentable carbohydrates, which can worsen symptoms. To reduce the fermentable carbohydrates that cause gas and bloating, consider soaking beans overnight prior to cooking. Soaking helps to leach out some of the oligosaccharides, the carbohydrates that are difficult to digest. When ready to cook, use fresh water instead of the soaking water, and cook the beans slowly over a longer period of

time to further reduce discomfort. Adding a piece of kombu, a type of seaweed, to the beans during cooking can make them more digestible and gentler on your stomach. Kombu contains enzymes that break down complex carbohydrates, making the beans easier to digest and potentially reducing the risk of gas and bloating. **Sugar alcohols** (e.g., sorbitol, xylitol, erythritol) found in sugar-free gum and diet foods can cause significant gastrointestinal distress.

Sugar Alcohols:
- **Sorbitol**: Often used in sugar-free products; provides a sweet taste without the high glycemic impact of sugar.
- **Xylitol**: Known for its dental health benefits as it makes the mouth more alkaline, preventing cavities.
- **Erythritol**: Generally well-tolerated and beneficial for dental health by helping to prevent cavities.

Gum and sugar-free treats often contain sugar alcohols or artificial sweeteners that can be problematic. While these sugar alcohols can be useful as a sugar substitute since they raise blood sugar less than white refined sugar, it is important to note that they can cause gastrointestinal distress such as bloating, gas, and diarrhea, especially when consumed in large amounts. Individuals with IBS or those sensitive to sugar alcohols should consider their tolerance and potentially use these substitutes in moderation.

By identifying and managing dietary triggers, individuals with SIBO and IBS can better control their symptoms and improve their quality of life. In severe cases, a Complete SIBO Cleanse Protocol may be beneficial, along with a hydrogen breath test (H2BT) to confirm the condition. Prompt and effective treatment is recommended to prevent further complications.

Proactive Health Management: To optimize health while managing inflammatory conditions, it's crucial to track how different foods affect your body, mood, and symptoms. Keeping a daily journal before and after consumption allows you to monitor any reactions or sensitivities, providing valuable insight into your individual dietary needs. This proactive approach empowers you to manage your condition and cultivate a deeper understanding of how diet influences your health.

Gut-Brain Connection and Nutrition

A healthy gut is essential for overall wellness. Emerging research highlights the importance of gut health in supporting immunity, mood, and even hormonal balance. Here's how focusing on your diet can benefit your gut and brain:

Supporting Gut Health

Probiotics and Prebiotics: Incorporate foods rich in probiotics and prebiotics to maintain a balanced gut microbiome, which is crucial for digestive health.

Calming Digestive Issues: Chronic issues like gas, bloating, and acid reflux often indicate an unhealthy gut. Address these by removing trigger foods and adding nutrient-dense options that promote gut healing.

The Gut-Brain Axis

Communication Pathway: The gut and brain communicate through the gut-brain axis. Stress can trigger digestive problems, and gut issues can impact mental health. Understanding this connection helps in managing both gut and brain health.

Reducing Inflammation

Identifying Triggers: Certain foods can cause inflammation, leading to digestive and other health issues. Eliminating these foods and introducing gut-friendly ones can reduce inflammation and improve overall well-being.

Boosting Immunity

Balanced Diet: A diet rich in dietary fiber, plant-based phytochemicals, and antioxidants supports a strong immune system. Combining this with other healthy lifestyle practices such as regular exercise, adequate sleep, and stress management can improve your body's ability to fight off infections and maintain overall health.

Sourdough Bread & Gluten

Sourdough bread, although wheat-based, undergoes a unique fermentation process by lactobacilli bacteria. This process aids digestion and can reduce the gluten content in the bread. Additionally, fermentation enhances its prebiotic properties, which are beneficial for gut health. However, gluten, found in wheat, barley, and rye, may trigger inflammation in certain individuals, especially those with gluten sensitivities or celiac disease, an autoimmune condition.

Below is an alphabetical list of anti-inflammatory, gluten-free grains, as well as gluten-containing and potentially inflammatory grains to help you make informed decisions regarding your sensitivities.

Gluten-Free, Anti-inflammatory Grains

- Almond flour
- Amaranth
- Arrowroot
- Brown rice
- Buckwheat
- Cassava flour
- Chia seeds
- Coconut flour
- Flaxseeds
- Hemp seeds
- Manna
- Millet
- Oats (ensure they are labeled gluten-free to avoid cross-contamination)
- Quinoa
- Sorghum
- Wild rice

Gluten-Containing, Potentially Inflammatory Grains

- Barley
- Bulgur
- Farro
- Rye
- Sourdough (contains wheat, but fermentation may reduce gluten content and inflammatory potential)
- Spelt
- Wheat

Understanding which grains to include or avoid in your diet can help you manage inflammation and support overall gut health. While sourdough fermentation can break down some of the gluten, it still contains wheat, which may cause issues for those with gluten sensitivity or celiac disease.

Sugar and Inflammation

Learning to read food labels is like deciphering a foreign language, especially when it comes to understanding the array of terms for sugar, from brown rice syrup to high-fructose corn syrup.

Sugar fuels our cells and triggers a reward response in the brain, often leading to cravings. However, excessive sugar intake can lead to addiction-like behaviors and serious health issues. It's essential to be mindful of sugar consumption to maintain overall well-being.

Consumption of refined sugars is associated with an increased risk of heart disease, diabetes, and obesity, all of which are linked to inflammation. While natural sugars found in fruits are preferable, moderation is key even with these sources.

Maple syrup, for example, is processed more slowly in the body, similar to eating an apple, rather than causing rapid spikes in blood sugar like white refined sugar. Maple syrup is water soluble, making it easy to digest and quick to absorb. It contains small amounts of minerals, such as manganese and zinc. In contrast, refined sugars like table sugar have a higher glycemic index, meaning they raise blood sugar levels more quickly after consumption.

Fructose is naturally present in fruits, where it is accompanied by fiber, vitamins, minerals, and antioxidants. This combination helps mitigate some of the negative effects of sugar consumption. The fiber in fruit slows down the absorption of sugar, preventing rapid spikes in blood sugar levels. While fructose in whole fruits is generally not harmful when eaten in moderation, high intake of fructose from processed foods and sweeteners can have negative health effects.

When grocery shopping, always check labels, as added sweeteners can be hidden in unexpected places. Being mindful of sugar intake is crucial for managing inflammation.

By recognizing the sources of sugar and how they affect your body, you can make better choices that support your health and help reduce inflammation.

Common Sugar Names on Food Labels

The following is a list of names for sugar that are common on food packaging. These names can often disguise the presence of added sugars in your diet.

- Agave nectar
- Barley malt syrup
- Beet sugar
- Brown rice syrup
- Brown sugar
- Cane juice crystals
- Cane sugar
- Caramel
- Carob syrup
- Coconut sugar
- Confectioners' sugar
- Corn syrup, corn syrup solids
- Date sugar
- Dehydrated cane juice
- Dextrin
- Dextrose
- Ethyl maltol
- Evaporated cane juice
- Fructose (especially in isolated form, like high-fructose corn syrup)
- Fruit juice
- Fruit juice concentrate
- Glucose
- High-fructose corn syrup (HFCS)
- Honey
- Invert sugar
- Lactose
- Maltodextrin
- Malt syrup
- Maltose
- Mannitol
- Maple syrup
- Molasses
- Palm sugar
- Panela
- Powdered sugar
- Raw sugar
- Rice syrup
- Saccharose
- Sorbitol
- Sorghum syrup
- Sucanat
- Sucrose (white table sugar)
- Syrup
- Sweetener
- Turbinado sugar
- Xylose

Inflammatory Sugar List

To help you identify and avoid the most inflammatory sugars, here's a separate list:
- Corn syrup, corn syrup solids (processed corn sugar)
- Dextrose (glucose from starch)
- Fructose (especially in isolated form, like high-fructose corn syrup)
- Glucose (simple sugar)
- High-fructose corn syrup (processed corn syrup with high fructose content)
- Invert sugar (glucose and fructose mixture)
- Maltodextrin (processed starch)
- Maltose (malt sugar)
- Sucrose (White table sugar)

By keeping this list in mind, you can make more informed decisions that help manage inflammation and support your overall health.

For a more in-depth discussion on Understanding Sugar and Glycemic Index (GI), please refer to (page 259.)

Mind & Body Nutrition

Principles of Intuitiveness

Transform your eating habits by embracing the principles of intuitive eating. Rather than mindlessly snacking or rushing through meals, slow down and connect with your food. Take a moment at each meal to appreciate its origin, texture, and aroma, much like savoring a fine wine. Consider how it will make you feel and anticipate its flavor.

Before taking a bite, savor the aroma. Then begin to bite and savor each taste, chewing slowly until the food becomes liquid. Pay attention to how you feel after each bite, and aim to stop eating when you feel satisfied, not overly full. Utilize the hunger scale to recognize your body's signals, ranging from feeling starved to comfortably satisfied. By tuning in to these cues, you can gain insight into your nutritional needs to make mindful decisions about portion size and knowing when to set your fork aside.

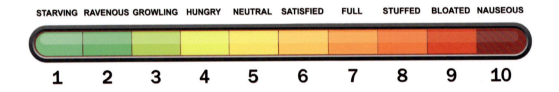

As you keep your daily journal, be sure to track your preferences and how different foods make you feel. Over time, you'll build a healthier relationship with food and discover more enjoyment in your meals. Remember, you are unique—what works for others may not work for you. Happy cooking, and here's to delicious, nourishing meals made with a wide variety of plant-based ingredients to help you feel your best!

DAILY JOURNAL

"When food no longer controls you, you can enjoy it without judgment, guilt, or shame."

Certified Brain Health Professional, Certified Health Coach, Gut Health Specialist & Healthy Cookbook Author ~ Michelle De La Mora

DAY: _____ DATE: _____

PLANT-BASED LIFESTYLE JOURNAL

DAY: _____ DATE: _____

By tracking your daily meals, activities, and feelings, you can better understand how your plant-based lifestyle influences your overall health.

Meals & Snacks: *What did you eat today?*
_____

Exercise: *What physical activities did you do?*
_____

Physical Well-being: *How did you feel physically?*
_____

Mental & Emotional State: *How did you feel mentally and emotionally?*
_____

Life Events: *Any significant events today?*
_____

Notes: *How did your food choices impact your physical or emotional state?*
_____

Water: _____oz.

Grocery Store Exploration Exercise

Now that you've absorbed a wealth of knowledge from the various sections in this cookbook, it's time to put your understanding to the test. This exercise encourages you to observe common shopping habits and reflect on your own food choices. After 30 days of eating clean using recipes from this cookbook, retake the exercise and compare the results. You should notice a significant shift in how you view food as medicine and how your taste buds have adapted to delicious, healthy options.

Task:

Take a trip to your local grocery store and observe the items in other shoppers' carts. This exercise aims to give you insight into common eating habits and purchasing behaviors.

Instructions:

1. Walk around the supermarket and discreetly observe the contents of other shopper's carts.
2. Record the most frequently seen food items below.

Common Food Items Observed:

Fill in the blank: _____

Analysis Questions:

1. **What's Missing?**
   - Identify any healthy food options that are noticeably absent from most carts.
   - Fill in the blank: _____
2. **Imagine the Impact:**
   - Reflect on how you might feel physically and emotionally if you regularly consumed the observed food items.
   - Fill in the blank: _____

3. **Visual Appeal:**
   - Consider what attracts you to the items in the carts. Think about aspects such as packaging, color, and branding.
   - Fill in the blank: _____
4. **Inspiration for Change:**
   - Based on your observations, what small changes could you suggest to others to improve their grocery choices?
   - Fill in the blank: _____
5. **Ingredients Check:**
   - Identify any items with a long list of unrecognizable ingredients.
   - Fill in the blank: _____
6. **Health Claims vs. Reality:**
   - Evaluate the health claims made on the packaging of the observed items. Are these claims supported by the ingredients and nutritional information?
   - Fill in the blank: _____
7. **Shopping Habits:**
   - Reflect on the balance between fresh produce and processed foods in the carts.
   - Fill in the blank: _____

Reflection:

Use this exercise to enhance your awareness of food choices and consider how marketing and presentation can influence buying decisions. Reflect on how you can make more informed and healthier choices in your own shopping habits.

Key Reflections:
- Reflect on the concept of mindful eating and its benefits.
- How often you see people making mindful choices versus impulsive purchases.
- Consider specific strategies you can implement and incorporate into your own shopping habits, such as creating a detailed shopping list, avoiding shopping when hungry, and taking the time to read labels and choose whole, unprocessed foods.

"When food no longer controls you, you can observe your thoughts, emotions, and pleasure around it without judgment, guilt, or shame."
—Certified Brain Health Professional & Health Coach Michelle De La Mora

The Importance of an Anti-Inflammatory Diet

Chronic inflammation is a common underlying factor in numerous health conditions, including heart disease, arthritis, diabetes, and even certain cancers. The good news is that you have the power to reduce the risk of chronic inflammation through dietary changes. An anti-inflammatory diet focuses on reducing inflammation in the body and promoting overall health. By incorporating anti-inflammatory foods into your daily meals, you can help reduce the risk of these chronic diseases, improve your immune function, and enhance your quality of life.

What Is Inflammation?

Inflammation is your body's natural immune response. When you get injured or face an infection, your body increases blood flow and sends immune cells to the affected area to help with healing. This is known as inflammation, and it's an essential part of your body's healing process.

However, while short-term inflammation is beneficial, chronic inflammation can be harmful. Chronic inflammation occurs when your body remains in a constant state of defense, even when there's no immediate threat. Over time, this can lead to tissue damage and contribute to various health issues.

Certain factors can contribute to chronic inflammation, including:
- Poor diet, particularly one high in processed foods, sugars, and unhealthy fats
- Lack of exercise
- Chronic stress
- Exposure to environmental toxins
- Sleep deprivation

An anti-inflammatory diet aims to reduce these triggers by focusing on whole, nutrient-dense foods that naturally reduce inflammation and support the body's healing processes.

By understanding the role of inflammation in the body and how diet affects it, you can make informed choices to support your health and prevent chronic diseases. This cookbook will guide you through delicious and nourishing recipes designed to help you embrace an anti-inflammatory lifestyle.

Turmeric Golden Paste: An Effective Anti-Inflammatory Solution

- *Anti-Inflammatory Properties:* Turmeric contains curcumin, a compound known for its powerful anti-inflammatory effects. Regular consumption of turmeric paste can help reduce inflammation and support joint health.
- *Antioxidant Boost:* Curcumin also acts as a potent antioxidant, which helps neutralize free radicals in the body. This can aid in reducing oxidative stress and promoting overall health.
- *Supports Digestive Health:* Improves digestion and soothe digestive issues, supporting the production of bile, which helps in breaking down fats and improving nutrient absorption.
- *Boosts Immunity:* Strengthens the immune system, making it easier for your body to fight off infections and diseases.
- *Enhances Skin Health:* Improves skin health, reduces acne, and promotes a natural glow.
- *Improves Mood and Cognitive Function:* Provides mood-enhancing effects and supports cognitive function, reducing symptoms of depression and improving mental clarity.
- *Supports Heart Health:* Helps cardiovascular health by reducing the risk of heart disease and supporting healthy blood circulation.
- *Versatile Use:* This versatile paste can be used in a variety of ways, from spreading on toast, to stirring into soups, layering over avocado as a snack, or adding to the Reishi Mushroom Turmeric Latte (page 226) or Golden Milk (page 225), making it an easy addition to your diet.

Turmeric Golden Paste

Ingredients
- ½ cup turmeric powder
- 1 cup water
- ⅓ cup coconut oil
- 2–3 teaspoons black pepper, effective for curcumin absorption

Directions

In a saucepan, combine turmeric powder and water. Cook over low heat, stirring occasionally until it forms a thick paste, approximately 7 minutes. Stir in the coconut oil and black pepper, cooking until the paste is smooth and well combined. Remove from heat and transfer the paste to a mason jar. Allow the jar to cool on the countertop before refrigerating. The paste can be stored in the fridge for up to 1 month.

Author's Note: For those new to turmeric paste, start with a small amount, about ½ teaspoon daily with food, on toast, avocado, or in soups. Gradually increase the dosage to 1 teaspoon as your tolerance builds. Note that taking it on an empty stomach may cause discomfort for some individuals. Consult with a healthcare provider before consuming turmeric paste, especially if you have health conditions or take medication.

Here's a guide to help you mix and match additional spices for your turmeric paste, which you can add along with the black pepper. This allows you to tailor the paste to your taste preferences while benefiting from their anti-inflammatory properties. Enjoy experimenting with these variations to discover your perfect blend!

Cinnamon & Cardamom: 1 teaspoon cinnamon and ½ teaspoon cardamom for a warm, slightly sweet flavor.

Ginger & Cloves: 1 teaspoon freshly grated ginger or ½ teaspoon ginger powder with ¼ teaspoon cloves for added warmth and spice.

Cayenne Pepper with Ginger or Cinnamon: A pinch of cayenne pepper with ½ teaspoon ginger or 1 teaspoon cinnamon.

Quick Craving Solutions

We all experience cravings, but understanding what your body really needs can help you satisfy them in a healthier way. Use this quick guide to discover smart choices and recipe swaps that will help manage your cravings and keep you satisfied.

HEALTHIER SWAPS FOR CRAVINGS

Sweet
- Water first. Sweet cravings can be a sign of dehydration.
- Opt for fresh whole fruit, apples with nut butter, dried fruit, smoothies, sweet potatoes, or Date Poppers—dates filled with your favorite nuts for a naturally sweet and satisfying treat.

Salt
- Craving salt may indicate a mineral deficiency. Replenish with mineral-rich options.
- Choose Sole (pronounced *so-lay*) (page 48), mineral water (such as San Pellegrino or coconut water), olives, pickled vegetables, or lightly salted nuts or seeds, including Roasted Rosemary Naked Almonds (page 96).

Creamy
- Choose smoothies, avocado, Chia Seed Pudding with Almond Butter (page 76), Berry Chia Dream (page 74), mashed sweet potatoes, or Cashew Crèma Mexicana (page 232) over tacos.

Crunchy
- Enjoy apples, frozen grapes, rice cakes, Popcorn Paradise (page 95), handful of nuts, Cali Almond Flour Crackers (page 101), or raw veggies with Pistachio Mint Hummus (page 106).

Ice Cream
- Try a Chocolate Bananasicle (page 223) or frozen grapes.

Caramel/Candy
- Indulge in Salted Caramel Chews (page 220) or Salted Caramel Fondue (page 219).

Chocolate
- Craving chocolate can sometimes signal a magnesium deficiency, but can also be driven by stress, a desire for emotional comfort, or just a preference for the taste.
- To curb your sweet tooth, consider Luxurious Chocolate Masterpieces (page 216), Truffle Joy Bombs (page 214), Rocky Road Fudge (page 209), or Edible Maple Almond Chocolate Chip Oat Cookie Dough (page 205).

Carbs
- Craving carbs may indicate your body is seeking quick energy or more fiber. Opt for complex carbs to stabilize blood sugar and keep you full longer.
- Consider multigrain rice, quinoa, legumes, nuts and seeds, sweet potatoes, Aloha Kakahiaka Overnight Oats (page 79), or tiger nuts.
- Tiger nuts are nutrient-rich tubers that offer a naturally sweet, fiber-packed snack, perfect for satisfying carb or sweet cravings while promoting energy and healthy digestion.

The Beverage Oasis

Revitalizing Elixirs, Nourishing Tonics, and Invigorating Smoothies

Rose Petal Elixir

Yield: 1–2 servings

Rose petals are soothing and calming. They are known for their delicate floral aroma and antioxidant properties that promote relaxation and reduce stress.

Ingredients

- 2 cups water
- 1 tablespoon dried rose petals
- ½ lemon, thinly sliced
- 2–3 cardamom pods, lightly crushed
- ½ tablespoon maple syrup
- Garnish with hibiscus salt or hibiscus sugar

Directions

Bring the water to a rolling boil in a small pot, then add the dried rose petals, lemon slices, and crushed cardamom pods. Remove from heat, cover, and let steep for 5-7 minutes to allow the flavors to infuse. Strain to remove the rose petals, lemon slices, and cardamom pods. Serve warm, or pour over ice with fresh lemon slices and a touch of maple syrup or your preferred sweetener. For an extra flourish, garnish the rim of your glass with hibiscus salt or hibiscus sugar to add a unique touch to your elixir experience.

For a convenient alternative to cardamom pods, use ¼ teaspoon of cardamom powder. To enhance the flavor profile, add lavender buds along with the rose petals for a floral and earthy blend. For added depth and richness, infuse a hint of vanilla or include the warmth of a cinnamon stick or ginger slices. With its versatility, the possibilities are limited only by your imagination.

Sole

Yield: 48 servings (1 teaspoon per serving)

Sole (pronounced so-lay) is water infused with natural Himalayan salt. This ancient remedy is believed to support hydration, detoxification, digestion, weight loss, blood sugar balance, muscle cramp relief, and more. It is rich in essential minerals and trace elements that play a role in various bodily processes.

Ingredients

1 tablespoon Himalayan salt chunks
8 ounces filtered water

Directions

Combine the Himalayan salt chunks and the filtered water in a mason jar with a nonmetallic lid, as metal can react with the active minerals. Refrigerate for at least 24 hours, allowing the salt to fully dissolve.

To use, add ½–1 teaspoon of sole to a glass of water or in the Electrolyte Fruit Punch (page 49). Drink sole in the morning on an empty stomach to maximize mineral absorption. Refer to the Sodium Content Calculator (page 49).

Author's Note: The exact amount of sodium may vary depending on the type and concentration of salt used. Consult with a healthcare professional before adding sole to your diet, especially if you have high blood pressure or any other medication conditions that may be affected by increased sodium intake.

Electrolyte Fruit Punch

Yield: 1 serving

Ingredients

16 ounces filtered water
1 teaspoon Fruit Punch Stur Liquid Water Enhancer made with stevia
⅛–1 teaspoon Sole (page 48)*
Ice cubes, optional

Directions

Pour all ingredients over ice in a glass, stir with a nonmetallic spoon, and sip.

Sodium Content Calculator for sole in 16 ounces of water:

- ⅛ teaspoon of sole is approximately 60 milligrams.
- ¼ teaspoon of sole is approximately 120 milligrams.
- ⅓ teaspoon of sole is approximately 160 milligrams.
- ½ teaspoon of sole is approximately 239 milligrams.
- 1 teaspoon of sole is approximately 478 milligrams.

By adjusting the sole quantity, you can tailor the drink to provide the right balance of electrolytes for different needs and preferences. If your drink tastes salty, you've added too much sole; reduce the amount to avoid excess sodium.

Author's Note: Sole contains a range of minerals and trace elements, including some of the following:

- Calcium
- Copper
- Iodine
- Iron
- Magnesium
- Manganese
- Phosphorus
- Potassium
- Selenium
- Sodium
- Zinc

Chamomile & Pink Lemonade Kombucha Fizz

Yield: 1 serving

This refreshing and soothing fizz blends the tangy zest of Pomelo Pink Lemonade Kombucha with the calming properties of Organic Calm Chamomile tea, which features chamomile, hibiscus, spearmint, rose petals, blackberry leaves, sarsaparilla, orange, lemon balm, pineapple, and passion fruit. The result is a balanced, flavorful fizzy drink that supports gut health while tasting delicious.

Ingredients

- ¾ cup brewed Tazo Organic Calm Chamomile Tea
- ½ cup Synergy Pomelo Pink Lemonade Kombucha, store-bought
- Garnish with ice cubes

Directions

Brew the Organic Calm Chamomile tea according to package instructions and let it cool. In a glass, mix the cooled chamomile tea with the Pomelo Pink Lemonade Kombucha; stir gently. Serve chilled.

Author's Note: For those new to kombucha, combining it with chamomile tea can reduce potential bloating, offering a gentle introduction to this probiotic-rich beverage. The calming properties of chamomile enhance relaxation and digestive balance.

Pair with fresh fruit such as dragon fruit or pineapple for added flavor, and consider using rose petal–encapsulated ice cubes for a beautiful presentation. Enjoy your fizz as a refreshing way as a boost to your wellness.

Tiki Love Potion

Yield: 1 serving

This recipe was inspired by my grandson, Arthur Savage, a budding culinary enthusiast. From concocting "eyeball soup" at the age of two using plastic Halloween eyeballs and spiders, to experimenting with real ingredients at age three, his love for cooking has always been a fun adventure.

Ingredients
- 2 Bada Bing Cherries or Merry Maraschino Cherries from Tillen Farms
- 2 tablespoons cherry juice from the Tillen Farms jar of cherries
- Ice cubes, as desired
- 2 droppers full of SweetLeaf Sweet Drops Chocolate Liquid Stevia Sweetener
- 6 ounces San Pellegrino sparkling water

Directions
Layer the bottom of a large glass with cherries, cherry juice, ice cubes, and chocolate sweetener. Slowly pour the San Pellegrino sparkling water over the top, watching the bubbles dance, and enjoy.

Sparkling Chocolate Blueberries & Mint Elixir

Yield: 1 serving

Ingredients
1 lime wedge
2 tablespoons defrosted blueberries
2 tablespoons defrosted blueberry juice
2 rosemary sprigs
Ice cubes, as desired
2 droppers full SweetLeaf Sweet Drops Chocolate Liquid Stevia Sweetener
12 ounces San Pellegrino sparkling water

Directions

In a glass, squeeze the lime wedge and drop it in, if desired. Add the defrosted blueberries, blueberry juice, rosemary sprigs, ice cubes, and chocolate sweetener.

Slowly pour the San Pellegrino sparkling water over the top, and watch as the bubbles create a lively mix with the ingredients.

For the best results, use organic frozen blueberries. Scoop out ½ cup at a time and refrigerate in a small mason jar until ready. As they thaw, the berries will release their flavorful juices, which you can use along with the defrosted blueberries.

Sparkling Blood Orange Root Beer

Yield: 1 serving

Ready to indulge in the crisp taste of root beer that's both bubbly and guilt-free? This choice offers the satisfaction of root beer without the added calories and sugar, perfect for satisfying your soda pop cravings.

Ingredients

1 blood orange

Ice cubes, as desired

2 droppers full of SweetLeaf Sweet Drops Root Beer Liquid Stevia Sweetener

6 ounces San Pellegrino sparkling water

Directions

Cut the blood orange in half crosswise. Reserve a few slices from the center for visual appeal and place them in the bottom of a glass. Squeeze the juice from the remaining halves and pour it into the glass. Add ice cubes and the root beer sweetener.

Slowly pour the sparkling water over the top, enjoying how the bubbles dance as they blend with the other ingredients.

Fire & Flux

Yield: 1 serving

This invigorating blend combines apple cider vinegar, lemon juice, cayenne pepper, and sea salt for a quick and easy tonic with various numerous health benefits. Apple cider vinegar aids in blood sugar regulation and weight loss, while lemon juice boosts vitamin C levels. Cayenne pepper helps reduces inflammation and supports heart health, and sea salt helps balance electrolytes and promotes healthy skin.

Ingredients

- **2 tablespoons lemon juice**
- **2 tablespoons apple cider vinegar**
- **Dash cayenne**
- **Pinch of sea salt**

Directions

Combine the lemon juice and apple cider vinegar in a shot glass. Add a dash of cayenne pepper and a pinch of sea salt, then stir thoroughly. Cheers to good health and the natural power of this invigorating tonic!

Raspberry & Cardamom Smoothie

Yield: 1 serving

This refreshing smoothie perfect for a quick breakfast or as a post-workout refuel. Packed with nutrients and flavor, the addition of cardamom and cinnamon adds a vibrant touch that enhances its taste.

Ingredients

- 1 cup unsweetened vanilla almond milk
- 1 scoop raspberry protein powder
- ⅓ cup frozen mixed berries: blackberries, blueberries, raspberries
- 2 tablespoons almond butter
- 1 tablespoon coconut oil, optional
- Dash cardamom and cinnamon
- Garnish with frozen berries, optional

Directions

Blend all ingredients on high for 40 seconds or until smooth. Garnish with a few frozen berries, if desired.

Electrolyte Tropical Smoothie

Yield: 1 serving

Recipe inspired by Michael Nuccio

Ingredients
- 1 frozen banana
- 1½ cups frozen mango
- 2 cups coconut water
- Juice of 1 lime
- Pinch of sea salt

Directions
Blend all ingredients on high for 40 seconds or until smooth.

Chaga & Hawthorn Berry Tea

Yield: 2 servings

Chaga is known for its immune-boosting and antioxidant properties, while hawthorn berries support cardiovascular health.

Ingredients

- 20 ounces water
- 4 Chaga chunks
- 2 tablespoons hawthorn berries

Directions

In a small saucepan, bring the water, Chaga, and hawthorn berries to a boil. Once boiling, turn off the heat, cover, and let steep for 30–60 minutes. Strain the tea, reserving the solids in the fridge for up to three uses. For a cold beverage, pour the tea over ice. For a hot drink, rewarm the tea and pour into mugs. Sweeten with local honey, maple syrup, or a squeeze of lemon.

Lemon Drop Healing Tonic

Yield: 1–2 servings

Indulge in this refreshing tonic as you savor each mindful sips. Occasionally nibble on the invigorating ginger and turmeric roots to embrace their healing properties and infuse your day with comfort and vitality.

Ingredients

- 2 cups water
- 1 organic green tea bag
- 1 tablespoon ginger root, shaved, skin intact
- 1 tablespoon turmeric root, shaved, skin intact
- 1 lemon wedge
- ½ tablespoon maple syrup

Directions

In a saucepan, bring the water to a boil, then add the green tea bag, shaved ginger root, and shaved turmeric root. Cover and simmer for approximately 5 minutes to allow the flavors to infuse.

Once done, squeeze a bit of lemon into your tonic and add lemon slices for extra zest.

Pour into a mug, including some bits of the ginger and turmeric for added texture. Sweeten with maple syrup or your preferred sweetener, if desired, and stir to combine.

As you enjoy your tonic, occasionally nibble on the ginger and turmeric roots to benefit from their healing properties.

For variety, enhance your tonic with lime and mint, or replace lemon with orange. You can also add a cinnamon stick, star anise, or experiment with basil leaves or rosemary for different flavors.

Chaga Frappé

Yield: 1–2 servings

The coffee used in this recipe is a courtesy of Chuck Jones, CEO of The Lawman Rub Co.

Ingredients

Ice cube tray
40 ounces water, divided
3 tablespoons ground Bourbon Pecan Coffee by Lawman Rub Co.
4–5 Chaga chunks
1 cup Coconut milk
1 teaspoon vanilla extract
2 teaspoons cacao powder
2 teaspoons maple syrup
½ teaspoon cinnamon
Pinch of sea salt

Directions

Brew Bourbon Pecan coffee with 20 ounces of water and let it cool. Pour half of the brewed coffee into ice cube trays and freeze. Reserve the remaining coffee.

Brew Chaga chunks with the remaining 20 ounces of water. Bring to a boil, then turn off the heat, cover, and steep for 30–60 minutes. Strain the liquid into a mason jar and let it cool. Store the Chaga chunks in the fridge for up to three uses.

To make the Chaga Frappé, warm the coconut milk in a small saucepan over low heat. Whisk in the vanilla, cacao powder, maple syrup, cinnamon, and sea salt until well combined. Stir in 1 cup of the brewed coffee and ½ cup of the Chaga infusion. Mix thoroughly.

Assemble the Frappé by filling a glass with the coffee ice cubes and pouring the whisked mixture over the ice. Serve immediately.

For a delicious finish, top with coconut whipped cream and a dash of cinnamon and cayenne pepper. For a Frappuccino-style treat, mix everything in a blender until smooth and enjoy.

The Art of Breakfast

Culinary Marvels to Start Your Morning Right!

Cheesy Jalapeño Pop'n Breakfast Cups

Yield: 2 servings

Enjoy the cheesy, spicy flavors of this easy-to-make plant-powered breakfast cup! The pickled jalapeños add a kick, while the Mexican-style cheese shreds melt into gooey goodness. Perfect for a quick breakfast, brunch, or anytime you're craving a savory meal.

Ingredients

- 2 teaspoons butter
- 1 cup JUST Egg
- ¼ teaspoon Mexican Fiesta Seasoning by Frontier Co-Op
- ¼ cup Mexican style cheese shreds
- ¼ teaspoon aluminum-free baking powder
- 2 slices Maple-Smoked Plant Ribbons (page 238)
- 6 pickled jalapeños

Directions

Grease two 4-inch ramekins with butter and set aside. In a small bowl, whisk together JUST Egg, Mexican Fiesta seasoning, cheese shreds, and baking powder. Pour the mixture into the ramekins and top with Plant Ribbons and jalapeños. Bake in a toaster oven at 375°F for 20 minutes. Carefully remove the ramekins using oven mitts and let them cool for a minute or two before serving.

Author's Note: You can choose to use Eggplant Bacon (page 241) instead of Maple-Smoked Plant Ribbons made with rice paper.

For variety, try adding ingredients such as diced bell peppers, chopped spinach, mushrooms, or fresh herbs and spices.

Easy Skillet Breakfast Potatoes

Yield: 2 servings

Ingredients

2 golden potatoes, diced
3 tablespoons avocado oil, or preferred oil
4 garlic cloves, minced
½ white onion, minced
¼ teaspoon smoked paprika
¼ teaspoon red pepper flakes
⅛ teaspoon sea salt
Garnish ideas: Pico de Gallo (page 237), plant-based sour cream, Nutty Parmesan (page 233), and/or fresh cilantro.

Directions

In a cast-iron skillet, sauté potatoes in oil for 5 minutes, tossing occasionally to ensure even browning. Add the garlic and onion, and continue to cook for an additional 10 minutes until the potatoes are nearly tender. Stir in smoked paprika, red pepper flakes, and sea salt and sauté for an additional 7 minutes, allowing the flavors to meld and the potatoes to become fork-tender. Serve hot and garnish with your favorite toppings, such as Pico de Gallo (page 237), plant-based sour cream, Nutty Parmesan (page 233), and fresh cilantro.

Experiment with different types of potatoes to find the best match for your taste and dietary preferences.

Sweet potatoes: Slightly sweeter and a lower glycemic index, perfect for those managing blood sugar levels. Sweet potatoes are also rich in vitamins, particularly vitamin A (in the form of beta-carotene) and vitamin C, and fiber.

Yukon Gold potatoes: Slightly buttery and rich in potassium and vitamin C, offering a creamy texture and more traditional potato flavor.

Purple potatoes: Packed with anthocyanins, these vibrant potatoes help combat oxidative stress and inflammation.

Each variety offers unique benefits, so feel free to mix and match based on your health goals and flavor preference.

Messy Loaded Almond Yogurt & Banana Nut Crunch

Yield: 1 serving

Ingredients

1 cup unsweetened vanilla almond yogurt

1 banana, sliced

⅓ cup freeze-dried strawberries

1 tablespoon dried cherries

1 teaspoon chia seeds

1 tablespoon almond or cashew butter

2 tablespoons plain slivered almonds

Dash cinnamon

Directions

Spoon a generous dollop of unsweetened vanilla almond yogurt in a bowl. Layer with sliced banana, freeze-dried strawberries, dried cherries, chia seeds, almond butter, slivered almonds, and a dash of cinnamon.

Explore a variety of toppings such as fresh diced apple, coconut flakes, pumpkin seeds, cranberries, or walnuts. Replace the yogurt with oat milk or almond milk and add granola for extra crunch. Another option: Use defrosted strawberries and blueberries as a base, drizzling their juices before adding your favorite toppings. This versatile recipe is perfect for breakfast or as a post-workout snack.

For a luxurious treat, I love starting with yogurt and a piece of Luxurious Chocolate Masterpieces (page 216), then layering with freeze-dried strawberries, creamy cashew butter, diced apples, almond slivers, chia seeds, and juicy defrosted blueberries, all finished with a drizzle of blueberry juice. Top with coconut flakes, a touch of Edible Maple Almond Chocolate Chip Oat Cookie Dough (page 215), a swirl of nondairy whipped coconut cream, and a cherry. This combination is like having dessert for breakfast; healthy, indulgent, and absolutely divine!

Berry Chia Dream

Yield: 1 serving

Ingredients

    2 cup frozen fruit, blueberries, strawberries, or mixed berries, divided

    ½ cup of the fruit juice from defrosted fruit

    ¼ cup chia seeds

    ½ cup sugar-free, nondairy yogurt

    Garnish with any nuts or seeds, if desired

Directions

In a saucepan, cook the frozen fruit over low heat for about 5 to 10 minutes, smashing them intermittently as they soften. Once the fruit has released its juice, strain the liquid from the fruit; you should have approximately ½ cup of juice. If you end up with slightly less, you can add some of the smashed defrosted fruit to the liquid, 1 tablespoon at a time, until you have ½ cup. Pour the chia seeds into a glass, and then add the ½ cup of fruit liquid over the seeds, stirring well. Refrigerate the mixture for 15 minutes. After chilling, remove the glass from the refrigerator and top with yogurt and the remaining smashed fruit, which should equal just over ¼ cup, plus 1 or 2 tablespoons. Finish by adding your preferred garnish, if desired.

Author's Note: Alternatively, you can defrost the fruit in the refrigerator overnight, which will yield less juice compared to cooking. When defrosted, you'll have around ¼ cup of juice at the bottom. You can mash the berries slightly to extract more juice. Use this fruit juice for the recipe, and make up the difference to equal ½ cup with your preferred plant milk, such as cashew, coconut, or almond milk. Combine this half cup of liquid with the chia seeds, refrigerate, and then follow the remaining instructions. You can use any remaining fruit in smoothies or as a topping for the Messy Loaded Almond Yogurt & Banana Nut Crunch (page 73).

For a tasty twist, try replacing the nondairy yogurt with nondairy Reddi-wip. You can also add sliced bananas, blueberries, almond slivers, and coconut flakes. For a protein-packed treat, consider swirling in some cashew or peanut butter.

Chia Seed Pudding with Almond Butter

Yield: 1 serving

Recipe inspired by Rachel Feldman

Ingredients

- ⅓ cup chia seeds
- 1 cup nondairy milk
- 1 teaspoon cinnamon
- 2 tablespoons almond butter
- 1 apple, cored and chopped
- 1 banana, sliced

Directions

In a serving bowl, combine the chia seeds, nondairy milk, and cinnamon. Stir thoroughly and let the mixture sit for at least 5 minutes to thicken. Once thickened, stir in the almond butter; it will remain in chunks, which is perfectly fine. Top with the chopped apple and sliced banana before serving.

Maple Almond Chocolate Chip Overnight Oats

Yield: 1 serving

Ingredients

½ cup gluten-free rolled oats
½ cup oat milk
1 tablespoon chia seeds
3½ tablespoons almond flour
2 teaspoons vanilla extract
1 tablespoon maple syrup
3 tablespoons Lily's dark chocolate chips

Directions

Combine the oats, oat milk, chia seeds, almond flour, vanilla, maple syrup, and chocolate chips in a serving glass or mason jar. Stir well to mix. Refrigerate overnight. In the morning you'll have a quick, nutritious breakfast that's as delicious as dessert.

Aloha Kakahiaka Overnight Oats

Yield: 1 serving

Ingredients
½ cup gluten-free rolled oats
1 teaspoon chia seeds
¾ cup unsweetened coconut milk
½ banana, sliced
2 teaspoons maple syrup
2 tablespoons unsweetened shredded coconut flakes
1 tablespoon sunflower seeds, optional
2 slices ripe mango, cubed

Directions

Combine the oats, chia seeds, and coconut milk in a serving glass or mason jar. Stir well to mix. Add the banana and maple syrup. Refrigerate overnight. In the morning, top with shredded coconut flakes, sunflower seeds, and fresh mango. Enjoy a quick, nutritious breakfast.

Feel free to experiment by adding your favorite nuts, seeds, cacao powder, or a variety of fruits such as berries, sliced kiwi, or dark chocolate chips. Elevate the flavor with chai spice or creamy nut butters. Ideal for busy mornings when you need a delicious on-the-go breakfast.

Spicy Chorizo Tacos

Yield: 2 servings

Ingredients

    1–2 tablespoons butter
    ½ red onion, slivered
    6 garlic cloves, minced
    1 Anaheim or bell pepper, thinly sliced
    ¼ cup soyrizo
    Sea salt and pepper to taste
    ¼ cup fresh parsley, spinach, or arugula
    2–4 corn tortillas*
    Garnish with Cashew Crèma Mexicana (page 232), Prosecco Pickled Jalapeños (page 242), or Chipotle Sauce (page 235)

Directions

In a skillet, melt the butter over medium heat. Sauté the onion for 4 minutes until it begins to soften. Add the garlic and Anaheim pepper, cooking until the pepper reaches your desired level of tenderness. Stir in the soyrizo, chopping as it heats for a few more minutes. Season with sea salt and pepper, then fold in the fresh parsley, and cook briefly until wilted. Warm the tortillas, then fill them with the soyrizo mixture. Garnish with Cashew Crèma Mexicana (page 232), Prosecco Pickled Jalapeños (page 242), or your choice of toppings. Additional options include lime juice, salsa, and cilantro

Author's Note: Add variety, try using the Spicy Lentil Tortillas from the following page instead of corn tortillas. They add a unique flavor and are a great alternative.

Spicy Red Lentil Tortillas

Yield: 2 servings

Ingredients
- ½ cup red lentils
- 3 cups water, for soaking + ¾ cup water, divided
- Pinch of sea salt and pepper to taste
- 1 tablespoon minced red onion
- 2 teaspoons green chili peppers, minced, fresh or canned
- 1 teaspoon sriracha
- 3 tablespoons extra-virgin olive oil, divided
- Garnish with Pickled Tofu Feta (page 244), guacamole, Castelvetrano olives, sun-dried tomatoes in oil, oregano, and/or salsa

Directions

Soak ½ cup red lentils in 3 cups of water overnight, allowing them to double in size. Drain and rinse the lentils. Blend 1 cup of the soaked lentils with ½ cup water, a pinch of sea salt, and pepper until smooth. Reserve the remaining ¼ cup water for adjusting the batter consistency. Transfer the blended lentil mixture to a mixing bowl and stir in the minced red onion, green chili peppers, and sriracha.

Heat a nonstick skillet over medium heat. Once hot, reduce to low/medium, between 2 and 3 on the dial, and add a bit of olive oil. Pour about ¼ cup of the lentil batter into the skillet.

For thicker, pancake-like tortillas, cook each side for about 3½ minutes, adding more olive oil as needed. For thinner, tortilla-like consistency, gradually add the reserved water to the batter, 1 tablespoon at a time, until desired thinness is reached. Cook these thinner tortillas for about 2 to 3 minutes per side. Top with your favorite garnish as is, or use them as a substitute for any recipe that calls for tortillas.

For a spicier, more aromatic flavor, mix ½ teaspoon chili powder, cumin, fresh cilantro, coriander, turmeric, minced tomatoes, and garam masala into the batter before cooking. Alternatively, for an extra touch, stir in a tablespoon of chopped cilantro and diced sun-dried tomatoes. For a straightforward option, use just lentils and water for a simple yet delicious wrap.

Savory Tofu Scramble on Sun-Dried Slathered Toast

Yield: 2–3 servings

Ingredients

1 block organic firm tofu
¼ teaspoon turmeric
¼ teaspoon paprika
½ teaspoon garlic powder
Dash cayenne
½ teaspoon thyme
½ teaspoon oregano
¼ cup organic low-sodium vegetable broth
1 tablespoon butter
2 garlic cloves, minced
¼ cup chopped spinach
¼ cup minced fresh parsley
¼ cup minced fresh green onion
Cherry tomatoes, halved
2 slices sourdough toast or Dutch Oven Cheesy Jalapeño Artisan Bread (page 254)
2 tablespoons sun-dried tomato paste
Garnish with lemon wedge and radish
Sea salt and pepper to taste

Directions

Drain the tofu and pat it dry with a paper towel. Wrap the tofu in a clean dish towel and press it between heavy plates on a cutting board for 1–2 hours to remove excess moisture. After pressing, crumble the tofu and set it aside.

In a small bowl, whisk together turmeric, paprika, garlic powder, cayenne, thyme, oregano, and vegetable broth. Set aside.

Continued…

In a skillet, melt the butter over medium heat. Sauté the garlic for 3 minutes until fragrant. Add the crumbled tofu and cook for 1–2 minutes until lightly browned. Stir in the spinach, parsley, green onion, cherry tomatoes, and the prepared broth mixture. Cook for 3 minutes, stirring occasionally.

While the tofu scramble cooks, toast the bread until golden brown. Spread the sun-dried tomato paste on the warm toast. Top each slice with the tofu scramble, a squeeze of lemon juice, and a few radish slices for added crunch. Add salt and pepper to taste.

Customize your tofu scramble by adding your favorite vegetables. Start by sautéing onions with garlic, then incorporate seasonings such as Mexican Fiesta or an Italian blend. For a unique flavor, try tamari, turmeric, bell pepper, paprika, and umeboshi paste or umeboshi vinegar, along with black pepper. Add chopped nuts, hemp seeds, or nutritional yeast for extra flavor and nutrition. Additional vegetables such as bell peppers, spinach, and mushrooms work well. Fresh herbs such as cilantro, basil, or parsley, along with a squeeze of lemon, can also brighten up the dish.

Sun-Kissed Capers & Squash

Yield: 1 serving

Ingredients

2 tablespoons butter or avocado oil
1 small yellow squash, diced
1 small handful capers, rinsed
2 tablespoons sun-dried tomatoes in oil, plus 2 tablespoons of the oil
Chili flakes to taste
Cracked black pepper to taste

Directions

Heat butter in a skillet over medium heat. Add the yellow squash and cook until fork-tender, about 5 minutes, stirring occasionally. Add the capers, sun-dried tomatoes, and sun-dried tomato oil. Cook for an additional 3–5 minutes until browned. Season with chili flakes and cracked black pepper. The capers provide enough salt, so it's not necessary to add any.

For variations, replace yellow squash with zucchini, or add fresh herbs such as basil, oregano, or thyme. For extra flavor, sauté with onions, garlic, or both. You can also top with spinach or arugula and let it wilt slightly before serving. Finish with a sprinkle of Nutty Parmesan (page 233) or Pickled Tofu Feta (page 244) for a creamy, salty touch. Experiment with different tomatoes such as cherry tomatoes or roasted red peppers to find your ideal flavor combination.

Nibble Bliss

Irresistible Bites to Savor Anytime

24-Carrot Gold

Yield: 2 servings

Recipe inspired by Scott Savage

Ingredients

- 5 carrots
- ½ teaspoon sea salt
- 1 teaspoon garlic powder
- ¼ teaspoon chili powder
- A few tablespoons olive oil

Directions

Begin by preparing the carrots: remove the ends, peel them, and slice into ¾-inch to 1-inch pieces.

Preheat the oven to 415°F. Arrange the carrot slices in a small cast-iron skillet. Sprinkle the sea salt, garlic powder, and chili powder evenly over the carrots. Drizzle with olive oil, ensuring the carrots are well-coated.

Roast the carrots in the preheated oven for 40 minutes to achieve tenderness and a slight char. Reduce the oven temperature to 350°F and continue roasting for an additional 15 minutes to deepen the flavors. The result will be crispy edges with tender, succulent insides.

Elevate this dish by pairing it with a generous portion of blue cheese or cream cheese, adding a creamy contrast to the carrots' natural sweetness. For extra crunch, sprinkle with almond pieces.

Blistering Shishitos with Feta & Fiesta Smoked Crème

Yield: 1 serving

Savor the smoky, charred flavor of shishito peppers paired with tangy Pickled Tofu Feta and a zesty Fiesta Smoked Crème. This unique combination is perfect for a discerning palate. See the idea section below for customizing the quantity of the crème.

Ingredients

- 2 tablespoons olive oil
- 16 shishito peppers
- 2 garlic cloves, minced
- ½ teaspoon lemon zest
- ½ teaspoon parsley, chopped
- Sea salt and pepper to taste
- Garnish with Pickled Tofu Feta (page 244) and lime juice

Directions

Heat the olive oil in a medium-sized cast-iron skillet over medium-high heat. Add the shishito peppers and let them char for about 5 minutes, turning to cook all sides evenly. Reduce heat to medium, then add the minced garlic, lemon zest, parsley, sea salt, and pepper. Toss gently to coat the peppers and simmer for an additional 2 minutes until they soften. Plate the peppers and scrape any remaining seasonings and oil from the pan over them. Finish with Pickled Tofu Feta and a drizzle of lime juice for a creamy, tangy kick.

Fiesta Smoked Crème Directions

Combine a 4:1 ratio of Plant Perks Smoked Gouda Plant-Based Cheeze Spread with Mexican Fiesta seasoning. Enjoy this creamy, smoky, and mildly spicy dip that perfectly complements the shishito peppers.

No-Crab Crab Cakes

Yield: 2 serving

Ingredients

1 can chickpeas, drained, rinsed
3 tablespoons plant-based mayo
1½ tablespoons Dijon or stoneground mustard
½ green apple, diced
½ lime, juiced
1½ tablespoons fresh dill
½ nori sheet, shredded
1 celery stalk, chopped
1 shallot, chopped

Garnish with vegan kimchi, fresh dill, and extra nori for a more pronounced "sea" flavor.

Directions

Blend all ingredients in a food processor until smooth or your desired texture is reached. Serve in an avocado half topped with kimchi, fresh dill, and extra nori for added flavor, or enjoy as a sandwich filling with your favorite greens and toppings.

Popcorn Paradise

Yield: 1 serving

Seeking a more exciting popcorn experience? Enter Popcorn Paradise! This tantalizing assortment of flavors combines the satisfying crunch of popcorn with the savory notes of peanuts, the sweet burst of dried cranberries, and the indulgent richness of Lily's dark chocolate chips.

Ingredients

- 1 single small bag popcorn by Skinny Pop
- 2 tablespoons dried cranberries
- 2 tablespoons peanuts
- 2 tablespoons dark chocolate chips by Lily's

Directions

Pour all of the ingredients into a large ziplock bag, seal, and give it a good shake to mix everything evenly. Enjoy!

Explore inventive ways to enjoy your popcorn. For a pizza-flavored twist, replace the peanuts, cranberries, and chocolate with pizza-themed ingredients. Sprinkle pizza seasoning and nutritional yeast over your popcorn. Add some toasted Vegan Pepperoni (page 250) slices from the toaster oven, and give it a good shake to mix everything evenly. Enjoy this delicious and unique snack idea that combines the best of pizza and popcorn!

Roasted Rosemary Naked Almonds

Yield: 2 serving

Almond skins contain tannins and phytic acid, which can hinder nutrient absorption and cause digestive discomfort. Phytic acid binds to minerals like calcium, magnesium, iron, and zinc, reducing their bioavailability. Tannins interfere with iron absorption. By removing the skins, you improve nutrient assimilation, reduce potential digestive discomfort, and minimize allergenic reactions. This simple step enhances digestion and nutrient uptake.

Ingredients

- 3 cups water
- ½ cup almonds
- 1 teaspoon extra-virgin olive oil
- 1 teaspoon rosemary
- ⅛ teaspoon sea salt

Directions

Bring the water to a boil in a pot, then remove from the heat and add the almonds. Let them steep for 60 to 90 seconds until the skins loosen, then strain and rinse. Gently squeeze each almond to remove the skins.

Combine the peeled almonds with olive oil, rosemary, and sea salt, mixing thoroughly. Roast in a toaster oven at 350°F for 8–10 minutes, or until golden and fragrant.

Author's Note: The almonds will continue to cook slightly after being removed from the toaster oven. Keep an eye on them to avoid overcooking, which can make them taste burnt.

For a tasty snack, enjoy ¼ cup of these almonds per serving, about a small handful. Be sure to chew thoroughly for better digestion. Experiment with different herbs and spices to create your own flavor combinations, such as garlic or pickling spices.

Coconut Date Energy Bites

Yield: 9 bite-size servings

Recipe inspired by Michael Nuccio

Ingredients
1 (16-ounce) package Medjool dates, approx. 21 dates
Pinch of sea salt
1 cup shredded coconut

Directions

Soak the pitted dates in warm water for 10–15 minutes to soften them. Drain the dates, then add them and a pinch of sea salt to a food processor. Blend until the mixture has a thick, cohesive texture.

Roll a tablespoon of the mixture into a ball, repeating until all of it is used. Refrigerate the balls for 30 minutes to firm up. Once set, roll them in shredded coconut until fully coated. Serve and enjoy your delicious energy bites!

Fire-Kissed Gouda Bites

Yield: 1 serving

Ingredients

6 Triscuit Fire-roasted Tomato & Olive Oil Whole Wheat Crackers*
12 teaspoons Plant Perks Smoked Gouda Plant-Based Cheeze Spread, divided
6 teaspoons sun-dried tomatoes, julienne-cut with herbs in oil, chopped

Directions

Arrange the Triscuit Fire-Roasted Tomato & Olive Oil crackers on a plate. Evenly spread 2 teaspoons of Plant Perks Smoked Gouda Plant-Based Cheeze Spread on each cracker. Top with a teaspoon of chopped sun-dried tomatoes, ensuring each bite is complemented by their tangy, herb-infused flavor. For an added crunch, consider garnishing with a sprinkle of chopped nuts or seeds.

Author's Note: For those with gluten intolerances, opt for gluten-free alternatives to Triscuit crackers. Almond crackers or other gluten-free options are great substitutes. You can also use the Cali Almond Flour Cracker recipe (page 101).

Cali Almond Flour Crackers

Yield: 1 batch, approx. 40 crackers

Recipe inspired by Lisa Stewart

Ingredients

¾ cup almond flour
⅔ cup tapioca flour
1½ teaspoon flaxseed meal
½ teaspoon sea salt
⅛ teaspoon baking soda
⅛ teaspoon garlic powder
2 tablespoons olive oil
¾ teaspoons maple syrup
3 tablespoons water

Directions

Preheat the oven to 325°F and line a large baking sheet with parchment paper. In a medium bowl, whisk together almond flour, tapioca flour, flaxseed meal, sea salt, baking soda, and garlic powder. Make a well in the center and add olive oil and maple syrup. Blend with a fork or your hands until combined. Stir in water and knead until the dough is cohesive, adding more water, 1 teaspoon at a time, if needed.

Place the dough between two sheets of parchment paper and roll to ¹⁄₁₆-inch thickness. Use a knife or cookie cutters to cut the dough into desired shapes and a metal spatula to transfer the cut crackers to the prepared baking sheet.

Bake for 15–20 minutes, or until golden brown. Baking time may vary based on thickness. Cool completely and store in an airtight container. These crackers are a delicious gluten-free alternative to any crackers. Enjoy with Pistachio Mint Hummus (page 106).

Continued...

Experiment with variations by adding ½ teaspoon culinary lavender, 1 teaspoon everything bagel seasoning, 1 teaspoon dried rosemary, or 1 teaspoon grated lemon peel to the dough. Before baking, sprinkle sea salt flakes on top, or add onion slivers, Eggplant Bacon slivers (page 241), or Maple-Smoked Plant Ribbons (page 238). For a sweet twist, consider incorporating dried blueberries into the mix and/or topping with rose petals immediately after removing from the oven.

Fuel Bombs

Yield: 8–10 bite-size servings

Where rich chocolaty goodness meets wholesome, nutritious ingredients, you won't be able to resist these irresistible treats! Perfect as an on-the-go snack or a post-workout indulgence.

Ingredients

- ¼ cup of nuts, your choice
- ½ cup almond flour
- ¼ cup oats
- ⅓ cup peanut butter
- 4 tablespoons maple syrup
- 2 tablespoons cocoa powder
- 2 tablespoons cranberries or dried cherries
- 1 tablespoon flaxseeds, optional

Directions

In a food processor, combine all ingredients and pulse until the mixture is mealy and well-combined. Scoop a small amount of the mixture into the palm of your hand and roll into a 2-inch ball. Repeat until all of the mixture is used. Store your Fuel Bombs in an airtight container in the refrigerator for up to a week.

Feel free to experiment with different types of nuts or add a pinch of sea salt for extra flavor. For a variation, try using almond butter instead of peanut butter.

Pistachio Mint Hummus

Yield: 4–5 serving

Recipe inspired by Lisa Stewart

Ingredients

1 (16-ounce) can garbanzo beans (reserve liquid)
3 tablespoons tahini
3 garlic cloves
½ teaspoon sea salt
¼ cup lemon juice, fresh squeezed
3 tablespoons olive oil
¼ cup lightly roasted and salted pistachios
5 fresh mint leaves
Garnish with extra olive oil, pistachios, and mint leaves

Directions

In a high-speed blender, combine the garbanzo beans, tahini, garlic, sea salt, lemon juice, olive oil, pistachios, and mint leaves. Blend until smooth. If you prefer a more traditional flavor, you can omit the mint leaves. Gradually add some of the reserved garbanzo bean liquid (aquafaba) while blending to achieve your preferred consistency.

Transfer the hummus to a serving bowl and garnish with a drizzle of olive oil, additional chopped pistachios, and extra mint leaves.

Simmering Soup

An Inventive Spoonful of Comfort

Creamy Chanterelle Soup

Yield: 2 servings

Ingredients

2 tablespoons coconut oil
½ cup diced yellow onion
3 garlic cloves, minced
1 cup sliced baby bella mushrooms
2 cups vegetable broth
½ cup chanterelle mushrooms
2 teaspoons thyme
¼ tsp sea salt
¼ cup pecans
¼ cup coconut cream*
Garnish with fresh thyme sprigs, additional chanterelle mushrooms, and a tablespoon of truffle oil, if preferred

Directions

In a large saucepan, heat the coconut oil over medium heat. Sauté the onion, garlic, and baby bella mushrooms for 5 minutes, until the onion is translucent and the mushrooms begin to soften. Add the vegetable broth, chanterelle mushrooms, thyme, and sea salt. Bring the soup to a gentle boil, then reduce the heat and let it simmer for 15 minutes to allow the flavors to meld.

While the soup is simmering, soak the pecans in a bowl of water for 15 minutes. Once soaked, ladle about a cup of the cooked soup, including some mushrooms, into a high-speed blender. Add the soaked pecans and coconut cream, and blend until smooth and creamy.

Pour the blended soup back into the saucepan, stirring gently to incorporate the creamy texture. Allow the soup to simmer for an additional 30 minutes, which will help it thicken and deepen in flavor. For a smoother consistency, blend the entire soup in batches and return it to the saucepan. If you prefer a slightly textured soup, blend only a portion. Taste and adjust the seasoning as needed.

Garnish with a few additional chanterelle mushrooms and fresh thyme. For an extra touch, drizzle with truffle oil just before serving.

Continued…

Author's Note: Use 1 can organic coconut milk in which the only ingredients are coconut, water, and guar gum. Each can contains approximately 1 cup coconut cream. Keep the can in the coldest part of the refrigerator until use. Do not shake the can or the cream and liquid will emulsify. You want to keep it separated. After opening, carefully scoop the cream from the top of the can and reserve the liquid for smoothies.

For a luxurious finish, drizzle a tablespoon of truffle oil over the soup just before serving. Other excellent toppings include hemp seeds, red pepper flakes, and nutritional yeast. If fresh chanterelles are unavailable, you can replace them with ¼ cup dried chanterelles or dried porcini mushrooms; soak for 15 minutes before adding to the saucepan. Feel free to explore additional spices or vegetables to customize the soup to your taste.

Orlando Tomato Soup

Yield: 2–3 servings

Recipe inspired by Janelle Orlando

Ingredients

1 garlic bulb
½ cup diced sweet potatoes or carrots
5 tablespoons butter plus a bit for sauté*
¼ cup olive oil*
¼ teaspoon sea salt
¼ teaspoon pepper
¼ cup broth (vegetable, mushroom, or your choice)
5 fresh basil leaves or 1 tablespoon dried basil
12 Roma tomatoes, sliced into quarters
1 yellow sweet onion, cut into quarters
1 teaspoon Organic Vegan Bouillon Chickenless by Ecoideas, optional
Garnish ideas: Fresh basil, sour cream, fresh green onion, nutritional yeast, and/or hemp seeds

Directions

Preheat the toaster oven to 400°F. Slice the top off the garlic bulb, drizzle it with olive oil, and wrap it in foil. Roast the garlic for 30–35 minutes until soft and fragrant. While the garlic is roasting, boil the sweet potatoes or carrots in a separate saucepan until tender, then set them aside.

In a medium-sized saucepan, combine the butter, olive oil, sea salt, pepper, broth, and basil, and set it aside.

In a large skillet, sauté the tomatoes and onion in a bit of butter until the tomatoes are soft and the onion is translucent and beginning to caramelize, about 10 minutes. Work in four batches to ensure even cooking, transferring each batch to the saucepan as it finishes and using an immersion blender to liquefy the soup with each batch.

Continued…

Once all the batches have been transferred, add the boiled sweet potatoes or carrots to the saucepan, then use an immersion blender to liquefy them in the soup.

Allow the soup to simmer for an hour from start to finish. It will turn a deep red and the dried basil will reconstitute.

Once the garlic is done roasting, carefully unwrap the foil, squeeze the softened garlic out of the bulb, and add it to the soup. Blend the garlic into the soup using the immersion blender until smooth. Finally, add the bouillon (if using), stirring until it dissolves completely.

Taste the soup, adding more broth or water, if needed, to reach your desired consistency. Ladle the soup into bowls and top with your favorite garnish.

Author's Note: If you prefer to limit or avoid using butter and oil, you can replace both of those ingredients with an additional ½ cup of broth in the saucepan. Sauté the tomatoes and onion in a small amount of broth at a time to prevent sticking. This adjustment will still result in a flavorful and well-balanced soup without compromising the texture.

The Creature Preachers' Black Cauldron Chili

Yield: 4 servings

Recipe by the Creature Preachers

Ingredients

- ½ tablespoon olive oil
- 3 garlic cloves, minced
- 1 yellow onion, chopped
- 1 large carrot, diced
- 1 red bell pepper, diced
- 2 golden potatoes, diced
- 1 large sweet potato, peeled and cut into ½-inch cubes
- 2½ tablespoons chili powder
- 1 tablespoon ground cumin
- ½ teaspoon dried oregano
- ½ teaspoon garlic powder
- ½ teaspoon paprika
- ¼ teaspoon cayenne pepper
- ½ teaspoon salt
- Pepper, to taste
- 4-ounce can mild green chiles
- 28-ounce can fire-roasted crushed tomatoes
- ¾ cup vegetable broth
- 15-ounce can black beans, rinsed and drained
- 15-ounce can kidney beans, rinsed and drained
- 1 cup frozen sweet corn

Directions

In a large pot over medium-high heat, sauté the garlic, onion, carrot, red bell pepper, golden potatoes, and sweet potatoes, in olive oil for 5–7 minutes, stirring frequently, until the vegetables soften.

Stir in the chili powder, cumin, oregano, garlic powder, paprika, cayenne pepper, salt, and pepper, cooking for about 30 seconds to let the spices become fragrant.

Add the green chiles, fire-roasted crushed tomatoes, vegetable broth, black beans, kidney beans, and frozen sweet corn. Bring to a boil, then reduce the heat to low and simmer for 30–45 minutes, stirring occasionally, until the chili thickens and flavors meld. Taste and adjust seasoning as needed. Serve hot with your favorite toppings.

Get creative and personalize your chili with your favorite toppings, such as chopped cilantro, diced avocado, shredded cheese, sour cream, jalapeños, lime, or tortilla chips. For an extra kick, add guacamole or hot sauce.

PhoMazing Soup

Yield: 4 servings

Immerse yourself in the PhoMazing experience, a flavor explosion that will leave you craving more. Awaken your senses and enjoy a satisfying bowl that might just have you reaching for a box of tissues!

Ingredients

    1 tablespoon sesame oil*
    4 green onions, diced
    2 tablespoons grated ginger
    1–2 celery stalks, diced
    1 (8-ounce) package mushrooms, diced
    32 ounces vegetable broth
    1 small bunch of baby bok choy, roughly chopped, core discarded
    2–4-inch piece kombu (seaweed), broken into pieces
    1 red bell pepper, chopped
    2 tablespoons tamari
    ½ teaspoon sea salt
    1 packet of rice noodles or Lotus Foods Organic Jade Pearl Rice Ramen Noodles
    A few slivers of yellow or white onion
    2 tablespoons white miso paste*
    A handful of bean sprouts

Directions

Heat sesame oil in a large soup pot over low heat. Sauté the green onions, ginger, and celery for 3 to 5 minutes until softened. Add the mushrooms and continue to cook for an additional 2 to 3 minutes. Pour in the vegetable broth, bok choy, kombu, red bell pepper, tamari, and sea salt. Bring the soup to a boil, then reduce the heat and let it simmer for 15 minutes.

While the soup is simmering, prepare the rice noodles or ramen according to the package instructions. In a small bowl, whisk the white miso paste into ½ cup of cooled soup liquid. Once the soup has finished cooking, turn off the heat and stir in the miso mixture until well combined.

Continued…

Ladle the cooked noodles into each bowl and top with the PhoMazing soup, bean sprouts, and slivered onion.

Author's Note: Sesame oil tends to smoke if overheated, so use low heat when sautéing. If you are sensitive cooking with oils that have a lower smoke point, consider sautéing with water, avocado oil, or coconut oil. Add the sesame oil over the top of the soup just before serving, once the heat has been turned off. Feel free to replace the miso paste with chickpea or organic soy, and substitute any vegetables to match your preferences.

Garnish with a touch of heat from sliced red jalapeño or chili peppers, a zesty lime wedge, fresh herbs like basil, mint, or cilantro, or extra bean sprouts.

Spicy Aztec Soup

Yield: 6 servings

Ingredients

10 ounces dry beans, such as 16-bean soup mix (discard seasoning packet)
6 cups water, for soaking
32 ounces broth of choice, vegetable or mushroom
1 (28-ounce) can fire-roasted diced tomatoes
1 whole dried pasilla chili pepper
1 whole dried ancho chili pepper
1 whole dried guajillo chili pepper
5 celery stalks, sliced
2 tablespoons avocado oil
1 large white onion, diced
1 (15-ounce) organic corn, with liquid
1 (4-ounce) can diced green chilies, with liquid
1 cup hot water, for soaking
½ teaspoon black pepper
1 tablespoon chili powder
1 tablespoon garlic powder
1 tablespoon Mexican Fiesta seasoning
1 teaspoon paprika
1 teaspoon cumin
1 teaspoon dried Mexican oregano
1 tablespoon epazote spice
1 teaspoon sea salt
Garnish with tortilla strips, fresh cilantro, and lime wedge

Directions

Soak the beans overnight in 6 cups of water to help them soften and absorb moisture. Drain and rinse. Place them in a Dutch oven with the broth and fire-roasted tomatoes. Heat the soup to a boil.

Continued...

Soak the dried pasilla, ancho, and guajillo chili peppers in 1 cup of hot water for 20 minutes or longer while you prepare your ingredients. Reserve the soaking water to use if you need to thin the soup later.

Add the sliced celery to the Dutch oven. For extra depth of flavor, you can caramelize the diced onion if you like. Heat avocado oil in a skillet over medium heat and sauté the onion for 10 minutes, stirring occasionally, until it starts to caramelize. Add the onion, corn (with liquid), green chilies (with liquid), and all the seasonings (except sea salt) to the soup pot.

Once the soup reaches a boil, cover and simmer, keeping the lid on to allow pressure to build and the beans to soften. Avoid lifting the lid for at least 1½ to 2 hours, as doing so may result in tough, undercooked beans.

After 1½ to 2 hours of cooking, uncover the pot and stir the beans to check for tenderness. Add the sea salt to taste, stir, and adjust any additional seasonings as needed. Re-cover and continue cooking for another 30 minutes, checking every 30 minutes until the beans are soft. It may take up to 3 hours for the soup to cook to perfection, but it's worth the wait!

For a creamy texture, blend the Spicy Aztec Soup in batches using a high-speed blender until smooth, or leave it chunky if preferred. Serve in bowls topped with a dollop of sour cream, slices of creamy avocado, crispy tortilla chips, chili flakes for an added kick, jalapeño slices, fresh cilantro, and a splash of lime juice.

Spicy Cinnamon & Coffee Chili

Yield: 6 + servings

The coffee used in this recipe is a courtesy of Chuck Jones, CEO of The Lawman Rub Co.

Ingredients

2 tablespoons avocado oil or butter

½ yellow onion, diced

1 celery stalk, diced

1 red bell pepper, diced

2 (14.5-ounce) cans Escalon 6 in 1 peeled ground tomatoes with added extra-heavy puree

1 chipotle pepper in adobo sauce + 1 teaspoon adobo sauce from the can

3 garlic cloves, minced

1 teaspoon paprika

3 bay leaves

1 cinnamon stick or 1 teaspoon cinnamon

1 teaspoon coriander seeds

3 cans red kidney beans, with liquid

1 can organic corn, with liquid

1 teaspoon coriander

2 teaspoons garlic powder

1 teaspoon cumin, optional

2 tablespoons chili powder

½ teaspoon smoked paprika

Pepper to taste

½–1 cup brewed Bourbon Pecan coffee by Lawman Rub Co.

2 tablespoons maple syrup

1 teaspoon sea salt

Garnish with corn, tortilla strips, olives, red onion, diced avocado, jalapeño, cilantro, shredded cheese, and lime juice

Continued...

Directions

Heat the avocado oil or butter in a Dutch oven over medium heat. Add the diced onion and sauté for 5 minutes, stirring occasionally until softened. Add the celery and bell pepper, continuing to sauté for an additional 5 minutes. Stir in the peeled ground tomatoes with added extra-heavy puree, chipotle pepper with adobo sauce, and all the remaining ingredients except the coffee, maple syrup, and sea salt. Stir to combine. Cover and reduce the heat to low, allowing the chili to simmer for approximately 1 hour while stirring occasionally.

When done, gradually pour in the brewed coffee, maple syrup, and sea salt, adjusting to taste. Stir well and cook uncovered for an additional 30 minutes. Serve the chili hot, garnished with your favorite toppings.

This versatile recipe allows for various adjustments. Swap the red kidney beans for your favorites or try a mix of tricolored beans for added variety. You can also omit the corn, bell pepper, or smoked paprika based on your flavor preferences and dietary needs. For a meaty texture, cook ½ to 1 pound of Beyond Meat Plant-Based Ground Beef after sautéing the celery and bell pepper. Break it up with a spatula and cook for 7 to 10 minutes until browned, then continue to cook the chili according to the instructions.

Midday Munchies Unleashed

Imaginative Lunchtime Temptations

Jalapeño Pizza Crunch Melt

Yield: 1 serving

Ingredients

2 teaspoons butter
2 slices of bread, toasted if preferred
2 teaspoons sun-dried tomato paste
½ teaspoon pizza seasoning
6 slices pepperoni*
6 slices pickled jalapeños*
2–3 red onion slivers
4 spinach leaves
1–2 tomato slices
2–3 tablespoons mozzarella

Directions

Fire up your George Foreman grill or panini grill. Spread butter on one side of each slice of bread and sun-dried tomato paste on the opposite side. Sprinkle the tomato paste side with pizza seasoning, then layer with pepperoni, jalapeños, red onion slivers, spinach leaves, tomato slices, and mozzarella.

Top with the second slice of bread, with the sun-dried tomato paste side facing the fillings and the buttered side facing out. Grill for about 3½ minutes, or until the bread is golden and crispy and the mozzarella is melted. Slice and serve with a bowl of tomato soup for a comforting meal.

Author's Note: When choosing jalapeños, check the ingredient list for additives like calcium chloride. For a healthier option with a great crunch, use organic jalapeños with minimal ingredients or make your own. You can find the Prosecco Pickled Jalapeños recipe on page 242. For a plant-based alternative to pepperoni, try the homemade Vegan Pepperoni (page 250), or opt for a smoky substitute such as Maple-Smoked Plant Ribbons (page 238) or Eggplant Bacon (page 241).

Continued…

Discover your own unique crunch melt by combining your favorite ingredients into a grilled sandwich. Experiment with options such as mushrooms, marinated red bell peppers, sliced pickle chips, artichoke hearts, arugula, Pickled Tofu Feta (page 244), olives, or any other toppings you desire. Unleash your creativity and enjoy the customizable crunch melt experience.

Creamy Caprese Seduction

Yield: 4–5 servings of Cashew Cheese Sauce; 1 serving of salad

Indulge in the mouthwatering Creamy Caprese Seduction, a dish that blends rich, creamy cashew cheese with vibrant, fresh ingredients. This enticing combination will have you savoring every bite and coming back for more.

Ingredients for Cashew Cheese Sauce

1¼ cups raw cashews, soaked overnight, drained
2½ tablespoons fresh lemon juice
2 large garlic cloves
¼ teaspoon sea salt
¼ cup + 2 tablespoons water
1½ tablespoon nutritional yeast*

Ingredients for Salad

Bed of arugula
2 medium Campari tomatoes, sliced
3–4 Sunset Sugar Bomb grape tomatoes on the vine, sliced or whole
4 whole sun-dried tomatoes packed in oil
8+ extra-large basil leaves, sliced
¼ teaspoon fresh or dried thyme
Black pepper to taste
1 tablespoon olive oil

Directions

For the Cashew Cheese Sauce, blend soaked and drained cashews, fresh lemon juice, garlic cloves, sea salt, water, and nutritional yeast in a high-speed blender or using the Twister Jar attachment for the Blendtec. Pause occasionally to scrape down the sides for an even consistency. Blend until creamy. Store the sauce in an airtight container in the refrigerator while you prepare the salad; it will stay fresh for up to 5 days.

Continued...

To assemble the salad, start with a bed of peppery arugula. Add the juicy Campari tomatoes, Sugar Bomb grape tomatoes, and sun-dried tomatoes packed in oil. Generously drizzle with the creamy Cashew Cheese Sauce, then finish with fresh basil leaves, a sprinkle of thyme, a pinch of black pepper, and a drizzle of olive oil.

Author's Note: Nutritional yeast is optional but highly recommended. It adds a subtle yellow color and a cheesy, nutty flavor to the cashew cheese sauce. The sauce shown (as pictured) is white as it does not include nutritional yeast. Adding it will deepen the flavor and enhance the overall taste of the dish.

Feeling adventurous? Discover how to transform your cheese sauce into irresistible Ricotta Balls with a touch of potato starch. Simply add 3 tablespoons of potato starch to the pre-made Cashew Cheese Sauce in a small saucepan. Heat over medium, stirring continuously until the mixture thickens into a solid texture. Shape the thickened cheese into Ricotta Balls—perfection is optional. For a firmer texture, submerge the Ricotta Balls in an ice bath for about a minute. These charming additions are perfect for topping pizzas, enhancing burgers, or adding a delicious touch to any dish you like.

Zen Garden Salad with Sesame-Lime Dressing

Yield: 2 Servings

The photograph on page 131 showcases a creative variation of the Zen Garden Salad, featuring different vegetables from the idea section. Feel free to mix and match these vegetables to craft your own unique version of the salad!

Ingredients for Sesame-Lime Dressing

2 tablespoons tamari
1½ tablespoons white balsamic vinegar
1 tablespoon toasted sesame oil
1 tablespoon maple syrup
1½ tablespoons fresh lime juice
2 garlic cloves, minced
1 teaspoon grated fresh ginger
1 teaspoon organic sriracha by Sky Valley
1 green onion, sliced or minced

Ingredients for Salad

4 cups lettuce or lettuce and cabbage blend, chopped
½ cup cilantro leaves, roughly chopped
2 celery stalks, thinly sliced
½ cup carrots, julienne-cut
¼ cup crispy onions
¼ cup peanuts, chopped or whole
¼ cup crispy jalapeños, optional
¼ cup frozen edamame beans, defrosted in warm water

Directions

Whisk the tamari, white balsamic vinegar, toasted sesame oil, maple syrup, lime juice, garlic, ginger, sriracha, and green onion in a small bowl. Transfer the dressing into an airtight container

Continued...

and refrigerate while you assemble the Zen Garden Salad. Combine the salad ingredients in a large bowl and toss until well mixed. Divide into two serving bowls, drizzle with the dressing, and serve.

Adjust the vinegar and lime juice to your taste. Personalize the Zen Garden Salad with your favorite vegetables. Consider adding shaved red cabbage, quinoa, cucumber, bell pepper, cilantro, and red onion. Salads can be boring, but not this one! Switch up the ingredients each time to keep it exciting and fresh.

Spicy Mango Salad

Yield: 2 servings

Kimchi is rich in probiotics, particularly lactobacillus, which help balance the gut microbiome. Regularly incorporating kimchi into your diet can boost digestion, strengthen your immune system, and combat inflammation. Its high fiber content also supports a healthy digestive tract, making kimchi an excellent choice for promoting gut health.

Ingredients for Spicy Kimchi Dressing
- ½ cup vegan kimchi, store-bought
- 2 tablespoons vegan kimchi brine
- 2 tablespoons sesame oil
- ⅓ cup apple juice, juiced or store-bought

Ingredients for Salad
- 4 cups mixed greens
- 2 tablespoons extra-virgin olive oil
- ½ avocado, sliced
- Pinch of sea salt, on avocado only
- ½ mango, sliced
- 2-inch English cucumber, diced
- Pinch of broccoli sprouts
- Cracked pepper to taste

Directions

To prepare the Spicy Kimchi Dressing, blend the vegan kimchi, kimchi brine, sesame oil, and apple juice in a high-speed blender until smooth, then set aside. Just before serving, toss the mixed greens with the extra-virgin olive oil. Spread a layer of the dressing on each of two serving plates, reserving some for a final drizzle. Arrange the mixed greens on top of the dressing. Artfully place the avocado slices on the greens, lightly salting them with a pinch of sea salt. Add the mango, cucumber, and broccoli sprouts. Finish with a sprinkle of cracked pepper and a final drizzle of the Spicy Kimchi Dressing. Serve fresh for the best taste and texture.

Crispy Garden Rolls with Hoisin Glazed Dipping Sauce

Yield: 6 rolls

Ingredients for Hoisin Glazed Dipping Sauce

¼ cups light tamari

2 tablespoons peanut butter

2 tablespoons maple syrup

1 tablespoon white balsamic vinegar

1 tablespoon toasted sesame oil

1 teaspoon organic sriracha by Sky Valley

2 garlic cloves, minced

½ teaspoon ginger, grated or minced

¼ teaspoon Chinese five-spice powder

Pinch of sesame seeds, optional

½ green onion, minced

Ingredients for Filling

1 English cucumber

¾ carrot

1 yellow bell pepper

¼ red onion

Few sprigs cilantro

6 spring roll wrappers by Blue Dragon

6 lettuce leaves

Garnish with lime wedge

Directions

To make the Hoisin Glazed Dipping Sauce, whisk together the tamari, peanut butter, maple syrup, white balsamic vinegar, sesame oil, sriracha, garlic, ginger, Chinese five-spice powder, sesame seeds (if using), and green onion in a small bowl. Transfer the sauce into an airtight container and refrigerate while you assemble the garden rolls.

Continued...

Slice the vegetables lengthwise into small, finger-sized strips and set them aside. Fill a large saucepan with water and warm it on the stovetop; then turn off the heat. Submerge one spring roll wrapper at a time into the warm water for about 10–15 seconds, or until it becomes pliable. Remove the wrapper and let any excess water drip off. Place the lettuce and vegetables in the center of the wrapper. Fold the lengthwise sides toward the center and then roll tightly.

Cut each roll in half and arrange them on a serving platter. Squeeze a bit of lime juice over the top and serve with your homemade Hoisin Glazed Dipping Sauce.

For a spicy kick, consider mixing a few drops of hot chili oil in your Hoisin Glazed Dipping Sauce or directly into the roll, or garnish with a slice of Thai red chilis.

Chilled Tofu Mac

Yield: 6 one-cup servings

Whether you're planning a get-together or a quick, flavorful snack, this plant-based combo offers a mouthwatering experience and packs a protein punch.

Ingredients

1 (8-ounce) package of Banza Elbows Pasta*
1 stalk celery, diced
10 cherry tomatoes, diced
¼ cup red onion, diced
1 ¼ cup organic silken medium tofu
¼ cup vegetable broth or water
1 tablespoon white balsamic vinegar
1 garlic clove
½ teaspoon garlic powder
1 tablespoon nutritional yeast
1 teaspoon maple syrup
2 tablespoons lemon juice
2 tablespoons Dijon mustard
¼ teaspoon salt
¼ teaspoon pepper
1 tablespoon dried dill
1 tablespoon pickle juice
Garnish with fresh parsley

Directions

Cook the Banza Elbows Pasta according to the package instructions. Once cooked, drain, rinse, and transfer to a bowl. Combine celery, cherry tomatoes, and red onion in a large bowl and set aside. In a high-speed blender or with the Twister Jar attachment for the Blendtec, blend the silken medium tofu, vegetable broth, white balsamic vinegar, garlic clove, garlic powder, nutritional yeast, maple syrup, lemon juice, Dijon mustard, salt, pepper, dried dill, and pickle juice until smooth and creamy.

Continued…

Combine the cooked macaroni with the diced vegetables in the bowl, and generously top with the creamy dressing. Gently toss to ensure the dressing coats the macaroni and vegetables. Chill before serving.

Author's Note: Banza Elbows Pasta is a gluten-free option crafted from chickpeas and prebiotics to support gut health and potentially reduce inflammation.

Let your imagination soar as you experiment with these exciting flavor options or discover your unique perfect blend.

Barbecue Mac: Add a touch of smoked paprika to the creamy dressing before blending for a barbecue-inspired flavor. Drizzle your favorite barbecue sauce over the top before serving for an extra burst of flavor.

Jalapeño Jazz Mac: For heat seekers only! Add diced pickled jalapeños to the prepared vegetables, elevating the salad's flavor profile with every bite.

Citrus Crunch Mac: For a light and refreshing mac, perfect for a hot summer day, add fresh lemon juice and lemon zest along with bright raw veggies such as julienned or shredded carrots, yellow bell pepper, green onion, or other raw and crunchy vegetables.

Earthbound Mac: Explore the earthy depth of fresh basil, parsley, or cilantro, adding a well-rounded flavor profile.

Savory Umami Mac: Infuse an Asian flair by incorporating a tablespoon of tamari into the dressing, adjusting the sea salt. This savory addition will deepen the flavors and add complexity to the salad. Garnish with chopped seaweed and a sprinkle of sesame seeds and/or chopped cashews or peanuts for an added crunch.

Creamy Avo-Madness Mac: Achieve a creamier texture by blending half an avocado into the dressing, unveiling a whole new level of creamy indulgence.

Guilt-Free Cheesy Nut Mac

Yield: 3 servings

For a soy-free alternative, cashews offer a creamy and delicious base. Replace traditional macaroni noodles with chickpea pasta, like Banza, known for its higher protein content and lower carbs, creating a guilt-free, satisfying mac.

Ingredients for pasta

½ package of Banza Elbows Pasta (about 4 ounces)

Ingredients for Creamy Cashew Sauce

1 cup unsalted raw cashews, soaked overnight, drained
4 garlic cloves
2 tablespoons nutritional yeast
1 tablespoon fresh lemon juice
¾ cup water
½ teaspoon Italian seasoning
¼ teaspoon rosemary
½ teaspoon thyme
¼ teaspoon sea salt

Directions

Cook the Banza Elbows Pasta according to the package instructions. Once cooked, drain, rinse, and transfer to a bowl. To prepare the Creamy Cashew Sauce, blend cashews, garlic, nutritional yeast, lemon juice, water, and seasonings in the Twister Jar attachment for the Blendtec or a high-speed blender; blend until smooth and creamy. Mix in ½ cup of the prepared Creamy Cashew Sauce for every 4 ounces of cooked pasta and enjoy.

Want to elevate your mac further? Explore the delicious options listed under the Chilled Tofu Mac ideas in the prior recipe. Additionally, you can try incorporating roasted garlic, a drizzle of truffle oil, fresh sliced spinach, or slightly wilted spinach warmed in a saucepan for a few minutes. For a unique crunch, add dehydrated pickle chips. Let your taste buds be your guide.

Radicchio Rosa Salad

Yield: 1–2 serving

Recipe inspired by J. Marchini Farms

Ingredients for Dressing
- ⅓ cup olive oil
- ¼ champagne vinegar
- 2 tablespoons honey
- Juice of 1 orange
- Zest of 1 orange or blood orange

Ingredients for Salad
- 3 heads radicchio rosa
- 1 orange or blood orange, peeled and thinly sliced
- 1 cup pomegranate seeds
- 1 small bunch carrots, shaved

Directions

In a small bowl, whisk together the olive oil, champagne vinegar, honey, orange juice, and citrus zest to make the dressing. Tear the radicchio and arrange it on a plate. Layer with orange or blood orange slices, pomegranate seeds, and shaved carrots. Drizzle with the dressing and serve immediately.

Ganis's Greek Salad

Yield: 1–2 serving

Recipe inspired by Sandra Ganis

Ingredients for Dressing
- ¼ cup extra-virgin olive oil
- 3 tablespoons red wine vinegar
- 1 garlic clove, minced
- ½ teaspoon dried oregano
- ¼ teaspoon sea salt
- Freshly cracked pepper to taste

Ingredients for Salad
- 1 English cucumber, sliced
- 2 Roma tomatoes, sliced in halves or quarters
- 5 ounces feta cheese, cubed or crumbles*
- ⅓ cup red onion, thinly sliced
- ½ cup pitted kalamata olives
- ⅓ cup fresh mint leaves
- Garnish with dried oregano, fresh mint leaves, and cracked pepper

Directions

In a small bowl, whisk together the olive oil, red wine vinegar, minced garlic, dried oregano, sea salt, and freshly cracked pepper to prepare the dressing. Arrange the cucumber, tomatoes, feta, red onion, kalamata olives, and mint leaves on a serving plate. Drizzle with the prepared dressing and garnish with extra dried oregano, fresh mint leaves, and cracked pepper.

Author's Note: For an all-plant-based version, try Plant Ahead Plant-Based Feta Cheese or make your own Pickled Tofu Feta (page 244).

Garlic Mashed Potatoes & Sweet Corn

Yield: 2 servings

Ingredients

2 teaspoons olive oil
1 whole garlic bulb
Small bag of frozen organic sweet corn*
2 cups chopped golden or red potatoes
3 tablespoons butter
½ teaspoon sea salt
Pepper to taste
½ cup soy or cashew milk
Garnish with nutritional yeast and green onions

Directions

Preheat your toaster oven to 400°F. Drizzle the olive oil over the garlic bulb, wrap it tightly in foil, and roast for 45 minutes, or until the cloves are soft. Allow the garlic to cool slightly, then squeeze the cloves out of their skins into a large bowl.

While the garlic roasts, warm the sweet corn in a small saucepan with a bit of water. In a separate pot, bring water to a boil and cook the chopped potatoes for 15 minutes, or until fork-tender. Drain the potatoes and add them to the bowl with the roasted garlic. Stir in the butter, sea salt, black pepper, and your choice of milk. Use an immersion blender to blend until smooth or to your preferred consistency. Garnish with nutritional yeast and green onions before serving alongside the sweet corn.

Author's Note: While corn is generally well-tolerated, it can trigger inflammation in some individuals. If needed, replace it with another vegetable. Asparagus, green beans, or any vegetable of your choice make great alternatives.

White Cheddar & Broccoli

Yield: 4 servings

Ingredients

4 cups broccoli

2 tablespoons avocado oil

½ cup raw cashews, soaked overnight, drained*

1 cup water

3½ tablespoons tapioca starch

3 tablespoons nutritional yeast

2 teaspoons white balsamic vinegar or apple cider vinegar

¼ teaspoon sea salt

¼ teaspoon garlic powder

Garnish with Nutty Parmesan (page 233), hemp seeds, and red pepper flakes or cayenne

Directions

Drizzle broccoli with avocado oil and roast at 375°F for 20 minutes until tender and lightly crisped. For a lighter option, steam the broccoli to your desired tenderness.

While your broccoli is cooking, combine the soaked cashews and 1 cup of water in the Twister Jar attachment for the Blendtec or a high-speed blender; blend until smooth and creamy. Pour the mixture into a small saucepan and add the tapioca starch, nutritional yeast, white balsamic vinegar, sea salt, and garlic powder. Cook over low heat, stirring intermittently until the cheese sauce thickens. This process may take several minutes, so be patient. Pour over prepared broccoli and top with your favorite garnish.

Blazing Buffalo Cauliflower with Blue Cheese Crumbles

Yield: 3 servings

Barbecue Alternative inspired by Arthur Savage
  Experience bold Buffalo flavor perfectly complemented by tangy blue cheese. Serve with plant-based ranch dressing, tzatziki, or your favorite dip for a crowd-pleasing appetizer.

Ingredients
  1 head cauliflower, cut into florets
  1 cup unbleached all-purpose flour by King Arthur Baking Company*
  2 teaspoons paprika
  ½ teaspoon sea salt
  1 teaspoon garlic powder
  1 cup oat milk
  8½-ounce bottle organic Buffalo sauce in avocado oil by Primal Kitchen
  Garnish with fresh parsley and blue cheese crumbles

Directions
Preheat your air fryer to 400°F. Place the cauliflower florets in a large bowl. In a separate bowl, sift together the flour, paprika, sea salt, and garlic powder. Stir in the oat milk until the batter is smooth and well combined. Dip each cauliflower floret into the batter, ensuring it's fully coated. Arrange the coated florets on a rack over a foil-lined cookie sheet to catch any drips.

Cook the cauliflower in batches. Place a few coated florets in the air fryer and cook for 10 minutes. At the halfway point, either brush the florets generously with Buffalo sauce or remove them, dip them into the Buffalo sauce, and return them to the air fryer to finish cooking. Once cooked, transfer the florets to a plate and garnish with fresh parsley and creamy blue cheese crumbles.

Continued...

Author's Note: While this recipe uses white flour, which can cause inflammation in some individuals, feel free to replace it with gluten-free flour or omit the flour altogether (as pictured).

For variety, consider cutting the cauliflower into thick slices to create Buffalo cauliflower burgers or into smaller pieces for use in wraps or tacos. Experiment with various sauces like barbecue or teriyaki. Enhance the flavor by adding your favorite spices to the flour mixture or sprinkling the cooked cauliflower with herbs and spices.

At just three years old, Arthur's budding culinary tastes are already taking shape. He has developed a love for barbecue sauce, preferring it over traditional Buffalo sauce on his cauliflower bites. Take a cue from Arthur—embrace your creativity and let your taste guide the way!

Chimichurri Chickpea & Avocado Sandwich

Yield: 4 servings

Ingredients
1 (15-ounce) can chickpeas, rinsed and drained
4 garlic cloves
½ small red onion, roughly chopped
½ large avocado
½ cup parsley
1 red chili pepper, minced
2 teaspoons oregano
Pinch of sea salt and pepper to taste
2 slices of bread, toasted if preferred
Spring mix or greens

Directions

To refine the texture of the chickpeas and ensure a smoother consistency, wash and peel them. Save the liquid, known as aquafaba, for the Strawberry Fields Forever Donuts (page 256).

In a food processor, pulse the garlic and red onion until minced. Add the chickpeas, avocado, parsley, red chili pepper, oregano, sea salt, and pepper. Process until the mixture reaches the desired consistency. Spread the mixture generously over one slice of bread. Top with your favorite spring mix or greens, then place the second slice of bread on top to complete the sandwich.

For a fresh variation, consider swapping out parsley for cilantro and add 2 teaspoons of lime or lemon juice. Instead of blending the avocado into the mixture, slice it and add it to your sandwich just before serving. This prevents the avocado from oxidizing and turning brown, especially if you plan to refrigerate the leftover chimichurri. If you prefer, you can omit the avocado entirely. For a creamy chimichurri, replace the avocado with a bit of Follow Your Heart Vegenaise. The remaining chimichurri mixture is versatile and can be used in additional sandwiches, salads, wraps, or tacos.

Crispy Sourdough Bread Sticks

Yield: 16 bread sticks

Recipe inspired by Tennessee Killer Breads owner Dori Orwig
Utilizing sourdough starter discard, Dori creates versatile bread sticks perfect as appetizers or alongside soups and salads. Customize them with your favorite flavors and enjoy the satisfaction of homemade bread sticks. I've used grams here for precision.

Ingredients

- ½ **teaspoon sea salt**
- **150 grams whole-grain unbleached bread flour**
- **50 grams olive oil**
- **300 grams sourdough discard (see recipe on page 152)**

Directions

Combine the salt and flour in a bowl. Gradually incorporate olive oil and sourdough starter (page 152) until a dough forms. If desired, add flavors such as cheese, herbs, seeds, or seasonings directly to the dough, or wait until the end to roll each bread stick in your choice of seasonings.

Transfer the dough onto a floured countertop and knead for approximately 5 minutes until pliable. Divide into small pieces weighing approximately 30 grams each, and shape into tight balls. Using both hands, roll each ball into a cylinder, stretching outwardly while rolling, until you achieve the desired thickness and length. Optionally, you can roll these pieces in herbs, cheeses, or seeds to coat the outside.

Arrange the bread sticks on parchment paper–lined baking sheets, spacing them to allow for even baking. For a more pronounced sourdough flavor, let the bread sticks rest covered in plastic wrap for a couple of hours before baking. If you're short on time, you can bake them immediately.

Preheat your oven to 285°F. Bake the bread sticks for about 50 minutes at this lower temperature to achieve a perfectly crisp texture. Once done, let them cool completely on a wire rack before serving.

While it is advised to store bread sticks in airtight containers, Dori has found that using a bread stick holder keeps them crunchy for days without needing an airtight seal.

Sourdough Starter Feeding Schedule

Ingredients
560 grams all-purpose flour, divided
540 grams organic whole wheat flour, divided
1,245 grams filtered water, divided

Directions

Day 1
- Combine 100 grams whole wheat flour and 125 grams warm water in a clean glass jar. Mix thoroughly and place in a warm environment (72–75°F) for 24 hours.

Days 2 & 3
- Each day, transfer 75 grams of the mixture into a clean glass jar and discard the remaining mixture. Add 50 grams whole wheat flour, 50 grams all-purpose flour, and 115 grams water to the new jar. Mix well and let it rest in a warm place for 24 hours.

Days 4–6
- Feed the starter twice daily—once in the morning and once in the evening, allowing the mixture to rest for 12 hours between feedings.
- In the morning, transfer 75 grams of the mixture into a clean glass jar and discard the rest. Add 50 grams whole wheat flour, 50 grams all-purpose flour, and 115 grams water to the jar.
- In the evening, after 12 hours, transfer 75 grams of the mixture into a clean glass jar and discard the rest. Add 50 grams whole wheat flour, 50 grams all-purpose flour, and 115 grams water. Let the mixture rest overnight.

Day 7 & Beyond
- In the morning, discard down to 20 grams of the mixture into a clean glass jar. Add 30 grams whole wheat flour, 70 grams all-purpose flour, and 100 grams water. Repeat the same process in the evening. Continue feeding twice a day—once in the morning and once in the evening—indefinitely. Your starter should now be active and bubbly, ready for use. When it reaches its peak activity, with a dome-like appearance on top, it's perfect for bread making. Just before your next feeding, use the discard for your bread sticks or other discard recipes.

Pear Jam

Yield: 4-ounce serving

Ingredients

- 3 pears, peeled, sliced, and cored
- 1 cup fresh apple juice
- 1 heaping teaspoon white chia seeds
- 1 teaspoon fresh lemon juice

Directions

Combine the peeled, sliced, and cored pears with apple juice in a small saucepan. Bring to a boil, then reduce the heat and simmer uncovered for 1 hour. Use a handheld immersion blender directly in the pot to puree to your desired consistency, or transfer the cooked pears to a blender for a smoother texture.

Continue cooking an additional 20 minutes or until the jam reaches your preferred consistency. Stir in the white chia seeds and fresh lemon juice, which will thicken the jam and infuse it with citrus notes. Pour the warm jam into a 4-ounce mason jar, secure with a lid, and let it cool on your countertop. Store in the refrigerator until ready to use.

To serve, toast a slice of bread, spread it generously with butter, and top with Pear Jam. This treat offers a satisfying balance of savory and naturally sweet flavors.

For a new option, consider apricot or peach jam by replacing the pears with your fruit of choice. Black chia seeds can be used in place of white chia seeds, though they may alter the appearance slightly.

Elevated Evening Soiree

Seductive Nighttime Escape

Abuela's Fried Sopes

Yield: 7–8 servings

Recipe inspired by John Del

Author's Note: While deep-frying may not align with an anti-inflammatory diet, you can explore a healthier alternative with the Abuela's Baked Sopes recipe on the following page. This provides a delicious option for those who prefer different cooking methods. For this recipe, you'll need an oil temperature gauge and a 9-quart cast-iron Dutch oven.

Ingredients

- **8 cups peanut oil**
- **2 cups white corn masa**
- **1½ cups water**
- **1 teaspoon sea salt**
- **Lime juice**
- **Garnish ideas: refried black beans or Bold Border Sauce (page 182), shredded lettuce and cheese**

Directions

Heat the peanut oil in a 9-quart cast-iron Dutch oven until it reaches 400°F, using a heat thermometer for accuracy. Meanwhile, mix masa with water and sea salt in a bowl to form a dough. Knead the dough with your hands for 2½ minutes until well combined. For each sope, use ¼ cup of masa dough.

Lightly dust a cutting board with masa. Mold each portion into a smooth ball, incorporating optional flavors such as chopped jalapeño, minced garlic, or shredded cheese if desired. If the dough begins to dry out, dampen your hands and continue shaping. Flatten each ball between your hands, then press the center with a small cup to form a bowl shape about ¾ inch tall.

Carefully submerge a few sopes at a time into the hot oil using a fryer basket. Fry for 2 minutes for optimal crispy texture or 1½ minutes for a softer result. Do not exceed 2½ minutes to avoid dryness. After frying, remove the sopes from the oil and drain on paper towels. While still hot, sprinkle with sea salt and a squeeze of lime juice, if desired.

Continued...

Once your sopes are fried and ready, top them with the Bold Border Sauce (page 182) or create a savory Black Bean Mix by warming 1 can of drained black beans, 1 can of diced green chilies, and 2 teaspoons of Mexican Fiesta seasoning in a small saucepan. Add a dollop of this mix to each sope, layering with authentic textures and flavors.

Give each sope a distinctive personal touch by infusing authentic flavors into the dough. For each sope, you can add 1 chopped jalapeño, ½ teaspoon minced garlic, and/or 1 tablespoon shredded cheese, if preferred.

For the ultimate experience, garnish with your favorite greens and, Cashew Crèma Mexicana (page 232), or other additions such as cilantro, salsa, minced green onion, red onion, lime juice, and olives.

Abuela's Baked Sopes

Seeking a healthier option? Sprinkle the prepared sopes with sea salt and splash of water for added moisture. Brush each sope with peanut oil and place in a preheated 375°F toaster oven for 30 minutes, flipping them at the 20-minute mark for even cooking. Enjoy a lighter yet equally delicious version of this classic dish!

Golden Spice Puff Pockets

Yield: 9 servings

Introducing a delicious reinterpretation of the classic samosa! These savory Puff Pockets deliver a burst of flavor with aromatic spices and wholesome ingredients, all in a convenient pocket form. Perfect for snacks, appetizers, or a light meal.

Ingredients

- 3 red potatoes, diced
- 3 carrots, diced
- 2 tablespoons coconut oil or peanut oil + more for brushing
- 1 small red onion, diced
- 5 garlic cloves, minced
- 1 can black beans, drained and rinsed
- 1 heaping tablespoon grated fresh ginger
- 2 teaspoons paprika
- 1 tablespoon garam masala
- 1½ teaspoons sea salt
- 1 teaspoon cumin
- 1 teaspoon turmeric
- Dash cayenne
- A few sprigs of cilantro, chopped
- 9 TortillaLand uncooked tortillas*

Directions

Boil the diced red potatoes and carrots until fork-tender. Meanwhile, heat coconut or peanut oil in a cast-iron skillet and sauté the red onion for about 10 minutes. Add the minced garlic and black beans to the skillet, cooking for a few more minutes. Drain the potatoes and carrots, then add them to the skillet. Season with fresh grated ginger, paprika, garam masala, sea salt, cumin, turmeric, cayenne, and cilantro, stirring to combine.

Continued…

You can make as many Puff Pockets as you like or save the remaining filling in the fridge for up to 3 days or the freezer for longer storage. To assemble, place ½ cup of the filling onto one side of an uncooked tortilla. Fold the tortilla over the filling to create a half-moon shape. Brush the tops with coconut oil or peanut oil and bake in a toaster oven at 350°F for 15 minutes, or until golden brown.

Author's Note: TortillaLand uncooked tortillas contain wheat flour, which may not be suitable for those with intolerances. For a gluten-free option, use corn tortillas, chickpea grain-free tortillas, or those made from almond flour or cassava flour. Note that these options may not puff up as much. You can also enjoy the filling on its own, scoop it into avocado halves, or serve it alongside a salad. Experiment with different options to find what works best for you.

These Golden Spice Puff Pockets pair perfectly with Harry & David's Classic Recipe Pepper & Onion Relish and a squeeze of lemon juice. For extra flavor, consider adding red chili flakes, coriander, or your favorite vegetables. Both oven and toaster oven methods work well, but the toaster oven excels at achieving a perfectly crispy exterior. Feel free to get creative with your ingredients and techniques to make these Puff Pockets uniquely yours.

Barbecue Italian Beyond® Loaf

Yield: 6–8 servings

Ingredients

1 can tomato paste, divided
2 pounds Beyond Meat Plant-Based Ground Beef
2 tablespoons potato starch
1 celery stalk, minced
¾ yellow onion, minced
½ red bell pepper, minced
1 teaspoon thyme
1 teaspoon garlic powder
½ teaspoon black pepper
2 teaspoons Italian seasoning
2 teaspoons yellow mustard seeds
1 cup Italian-style panko
2 tablespoons butter, avocado oil, or peanut oil
2 tablespoons Primal Kitchen Unsweetened Classic Barbeque Sauce

Directions

Preheat your oven to 350°F. In a mixing bowl, combine half of the tomato paste, Beyond Meat, potato starch, celery, onion, bell pepper, thyme, garlic powder, black pepper, Italian seasoning, mustard seeds, and panko. Knead the mixture until fully blended. Grease a small glass casserole dish with butter or oil, then firmly press the mixture into the dish. Mix the remaining half of the tomato paste with 2 tablespoons of barbecue sauce and spread it over the top of the loaf.

Cover the dish with foil and bake for 1 hour. Remove the foil and bake for an additional 15–20 minutes, until the top starts to brown. Serve with a side salad or Garlic Mashed Potatoes & Sweet Corn (page 144).

Personalize your loaf by adding your favorite vegetables or substituting others to match your taste. Great topping ideas include a drizzle of extra barbecue sauce, hot sauce, caramelized onions, sautéed mushrooms, or fresh herbs.

Pulled Lion's Mane Slaw Burger

Yield: 2 servings

An irresistible burger featuring the hearty, exotic flavors of lion's mane mushrooms. Each bite offers a delicious combination of caramelized onion, meaty mushrooms, tangy barbecue sauce, and refreshing slaw.

Ingredients for Garden Goddess Slaw

- 1½ cups green and/or purple cabbage, sliced
- ½ cups carrots, shredded
- ¼ cup plant-based mayonnaise
- 1 tablespoon apple cider vinegar
- ½ tablespoon Dijon mustard
- ½ tablespoon maple syrup
- Sea salt and pepper to taste

Ingredients for Pulled Lion's Mane

- ¼ red onion, minced
- 3 teaspoons butter, divided
- 4 ounces lion's mane mushrooms*
- ¼ cup barbecue sauce of your choice
- 2 burger buns, toasted if preferred

Directions

To prepare the slaw, combine the cabbage, carrots, plant-based mayonnaise, apple cider vinegar, Dijon mustard, maple syrup, salt, and pepper in a small bowl. Mix well and refrigerate to let the flavors meld.

Sauté the minced red onion in 1 teaspoon of butter for about 5 minutes, until caramelized. Separate the lion's mane mushrooms into shreds, which will reduce to about ⅓ of their original volume as they cook. Add the mushroom shreds to the skillet with the remaining 2 teaspoons of butter and sauté until golden brown, about 3 minutes. Add the barbecue sauce, stirring well, and cook for an additional 1–2 minutes to blend the flavors.

Continued...

While the mushrooms and onion cook, toast the burger buns if desired. To assemble the burger, place a generous scoop (about ¼ cup) of the Pulled Lion's Mane onto the bottom half of each burger bun. Top with ¼ cup of the Green Goddess Slaw, add the top bun, and enjoy.

To elevate the Pulled Lion's Mane Slaw Burger, consider adding a variety of complementary toppings. Creamy avocado slices, tangy pickles, and fresh arugula can provide a delicious contrast in texture and flavor. Fresh or pickled jalapeños add a spicy kick, while melted plant-based cheese offers a rich, savory element. For a touch of sweetness, grilled pineapple pairs wonderfully. For an extra burst of flavor, finish with Spicy Garlic Aioli (page 234), or drizzle on a white balsamic glaze.

The secret to crafting irresistible homemade meals that outshine fast food lies in the layers of flavors, each topping adds depth and complexity, making every bite even more delicious and satisfying.

Author's Note: Lion's mane mushrooms, also known as *Hericium erinaceus*, are visually captivating and uniquely flavorful. Resembling a lion's mane, they offer a delicate flavor and a tender, meaty texture, making them an excellent choice for protein-packed, plant-based options. Beyond their culinary appeal, lion's mane mushrooms hold a rich history in Chinese and Japanese medicine and are believed to provide cognitive and neurological benefits. Incorporate lion's mane into your plant-based cooking for delicious and nutritious dishes.

Mangiameli's Family Spaghetti Sauce

Yield: 2–4 servings

Recipe inspired by Tony Mangiameli

This versatile sauce is perfect for traditional pasta and works beautifully over zucchini noodles or as a flavorful pizza sauce.

Ingredients

¼ cup olive oil
½ onion, diced
6 garlic cloves, minced
2 teaspoons garlic powder
2 teaspoons Italian seasoning
1 teaspoon black pepper
½ teaspoon parsley
1 (4-ounce) can tomato paste
1 (28-ounce) can Cento tomato sauce
1 (28-ounce) can crushed tomatoes
14 ounces water*
½ teaspoon sugar or 1 diced carrot
Pepper to taste
3–5 large fresh basil leaves

Directions

Prepare all ingredients ahead of time to streamline the cooking process. Preheat a large saucepan over medium heat. Coat the bottom of the pot with olive oil. Add the onion, minced garlic, garlic powder, Italian seasoning, black pepper, and parsley. Stir to combine and cook for 5 minutes, stirring often, until onion and garlic soften but are not browned.

Add the tomato paste, which serves to thicken the sauce. Stir constantly for 1½–2 minutes to avoid burning the paste, as burnt paste can ruin the sauce. Pour in the canned tomato sauce, crushed tomatoes, and 14 ounces of water to thin the sauce. Stir in the sugar or carrot at this time to balance the acidity.

Reduce the heat to low simmer, partially covering the pot to allow steam to escape. Maintain this temperature for the duration of cooking. Stir the sauce every 15 minutes to prevent burning. Avoid covering the pot completely, as this can cause the sauce to overheat and burn. Simmer for a total of 3 hours to allow the flavors to meld and develop.

Perform a taste test halfway through the cooking process to evaluate the sauce's flavor. Adjust the seasoning as needed, which may involve adding more pepper, garlic, or other desired spices. At this time, add the basil leaves, stir, and continue to simmer.

During the last half hour of cooking, taste the sauce again and make any final adjustments as necessary. If cooking on a Sunday, ensure the sauce is ready by 3:00 p.m., as Italian households traditionally eat at this time.

Author's Note: Adjust the water quantity based on your desired thickness: for an extremely thick sauce, omit the water; for a medium consistency, add 14 ounces water; for a thinner consistency, add 28 ounces of water.

Looking for a spaghetti sauce using only whole ingredients, not canned? Check out Giovanni's Spaghetti Sauce (page 170).

Why Use a Wooden Spoon

Wooden spoons are nonreactive, preventing any metallic taste from the acidic ingredients such as tomatoes. Plus, using one is an Italian tradition for making spaghetti sauce.

Giovanni's Spaghetti Sauce

Yield: 2 servings

Recipe inspired by Tony Mangiameli

This versatile sauce is perfect for traditional pasta and works beautifully over zucchini noodles or as a flavorful pizza sauce.

Ingredients

1 garlic bulb
¼ cup olive oil
½ onion, diced
2 teaspoons garlic powder
2 teaspoons Italian seasoning
1 teaspoon black pepper
½ teaspoon parsley
8 San Mariano or Roma tomatoes, diced
1 carrot, minced (approximately ½ cup)
5 large fresh basil leaves*

Directions

Preheat the toaster oven to 400°F. Slice the top off the garlic bulb, drizzle it with olive oil, and wrap it in foil. Roast the garlic for 30–35 minutes until soft and fragrant. While the garlic is roasting, prepare all ingredients ahead of time to streamline the cooking process.

Preheat a large saucepan over medium heat. Coat the bottom of the pot with olive oil. Add the onion, garlic powder, Italian seasoning, black pepper, and parsley. Stir to combine and cook for 10 minutes, stirring occasionally, until the onion softens but is browned. Add the tomatoes, and add the carrot at this time to balance the acidity. As soon as the garlic is soft, squeeze it into the sauce and stir to combine.

Continued...

Reduce the heat to low simmer, partially covering the pot to allow steam to escape. Maintain this temperature for the duration of cooking. Stir the sauce every 15 minutes to prevent burning. Avoid covering the pot completely, as this can cause the sauce to overheat and burn. Simmer for a total of 3 hours to allow the flavors to meld and develop.

Perform a taste test halfway through the cooking process to evaluate the sauce's flavor. Adjust the seasoning as needed, which may involve adding more garlic, or other desired spices. At this time, add the basil leaves, stir, and continue to simmer.

During the last half hour of cooking, taste the sauce again and make any final adjustments as necessary. If cooking on a Sunday, ensure the sauce is ready by 3:00 p.m., as Italian households traditionally eat at this time.

Author's Note: To deepen the sauce's rich flavors, I have added 3 additional basil leaves, 1 teaspoon parsley, and ¼ cup of Cabernet. The wine adds a beautiful depth and complexity to the sauce.

Cashew Basil Blitz

Yield: 2–4 servings

Create this incredibly versatile cheeseless sauce in just minutes with a food processor. Perfect for pasta, veggie dips, pizza, and more.

Ingredients

4 garlic cloves
¼ teaspoon sea salt
½ cup raw cashews
1 bunch basil, large stems removed
1 cup cold-pressed olive oil
Juice of ½ lemon
1 tablespoon lemon zest
¼ cup pumpkin seeds
¼ teaspoon cayenne pepper
1 tablespoon nutritional yeast
1 cup spinach or kale
Pepper to taste

Directions

Pulse the garlic in a food processor until minced. Add the sea salt, cashews, basil, olive oil, lemon juice, lemon zest, pumpkin seeds, cayenne pepper, nutritional yeast, spinach, and a pinch of pepper. Process until the mixture achieves the desired consistency, whether chunky or smooth. Transfer the Cashew Basil Blitz into an airtight container and refrigerate for up to 4-5 days. Avoid adding water, as it can affect the texture and flavor. If needed, adjust with additional oil.

Feel free to experiment by adding extra basil for a more intense flavor, kale for added calcium, or spinach or arugula for variety. You can also incorporate sun-dried tomatoes or other ingredients to suit your taste. Here are some delicious ways to enjoy your creation.

Continued…

For low-carb options, toss your Cashew Basil Blitz with zoodles (julienned zucchini noodles) and garnish with sun-dried tomatoes and nutty hemp seeds. Alternatively, use tofu shirataki noodles—but be sure to soak and rinse them thoroughly before heating in a pan with a touch of butter.

For a classic pasta dish, mix cooked spaghetti noodles (as pictured) with your Cashew Basil Blitz and top with fresh basil, Nutty Parmesan (page 233), and hemp seeds for added texture and flavor.

Green Spaghetti

Yield: 2–4 servings

Recipe inspired by Scott Savage

Ingredients

- 7 poblano peppers
- 1 (8-ounce) package Banza Angel Hair Spaghetti Noodles
- 4 teaspoons Cashew Crèma Mexicana (page 232)*
- 2 large basil leaves
- 1 teaspoon Organic Vegan Bouillon Chickenless by Ecoideas*
- ¼ cup spaghetti water + an additional ¼ cup for thinning
- 1 mini avocado or ½ large avocado
- 1 tablespoon butter
- 1 tablespoon oil
- Garnish ideas: nutritional yeast or Nutty Parmesan (page 233), chopped basil, red pepper flakes, and additional Cashew Crèma Mexicana

Directions

Heat a cast-iron skillet over high heat. Place the poblano peppers in the skillet, pressing them down occasionally until they are charred on one side, then flip to char the other side. This process takes about 10 minutes. Transfer the charred peppers to a glass bowl, cover with plastic wrap to trap the moisture, and let them sit for 15 minutes.

While the peppers are resting, bring a pot of water to a boil and cook the spaghetti noodles according to package instructions. Once the peppers have rested, remove them from the bowl and peel off some of the blackened skin. For a milder sauce, discard some of the seeds; for extra heat, leave them in.

Place the peeled peppers in a blender with 4 heaping teaspoons of Cashew Crèma Mexicana, basil leaves, the bouillon, ¼ cup of the reserved spaghetti water, and the avocado. Blend until creamy. If the sauce is too thick, add an additional ¼ cup of spaghetti water and blend again.

Continued...

Drain the cooked noodles and return them to the pot. Add the oil and butter, then stir until well combined. Pour the poblano sauce over the pasta and mix thoroughly. Garnish with your choice of nutritional yeast or Nutty Parmesan (page 233), chopped basil, red pepper flakes, and additional Cashew Crèma Mexicana.

Author's Note: Scott's original dish contains Mexican sour cream and a chicken bouillon cube.

Take your Green Spaghetti up a notch by preparing your pasta to perfection, then topping it with Rao's Arrabbiata Sauce. Garnish with a generous amount of Green Spaghetti Sauce, and finish with a dollop of sour cream. Twirl it all together with a fork and enjoy with a side of toasted garlic bread to soak up every bit of flavor.

Ratatouille

Yield: 8–10 servings

Recipe inspired by Catherine Sandoz of Nurse Cat, LLC

During the end of the summertime harvest, Catherine loves to usher in the new season of fall with a delicious ratatouille. This recipe is rich in flavor and dates back to the 1700s, where it was originally known as "peasants' stew."

Ingredients

- 2 red bell peppers, cored and seeds removed, sliced
- 4 heirloom tomatoes, quartered
- 3 shallots, peeled and halved
- 2 peeled bulbs of garlic, peeled, remove ends
- 1 jalapeño or chili pepper, remove seeds
- Olive oil
- Salt and pepper to taste
- 3 Roma tomatoes
- 2 Chinese eggplants
- 2 small yellow squash
- 2 small zucchini
- 6–8 sprigs thyme, leaves removed

Directions

Preheat the oven to 425°F. On a baking sheet, arrange the bell peppers, heirloom tomatoes, shallots, garlic bulbs, and jalapeño. Drizzle with olive oil and add salt and pepper. Roast vegetables in the oven for 35–40 minutes, then transfer the roasted vegetables to a blender and blitz until smooth. Pour the blended sauce into the bottom of a cast-iron skillet, spreading it evenly.

Using a mandoline or sharp knife, thinly slice the Roma tomatoes, eggplants, yellow squash, and zucchini. Arrange the slices into sets of four, one of each vegetable per set. Starting on the outer edge of the skillet, place each set of slices into the sauce, working in a spiral pattern toward the center. Bake for 30 minutes. Remove from the oven, garnish with thyme leaves, and season with additional salt and pepper to taste.

Cashew Crème Fraîche

Yield: 4 servings

Introducing a mouthwatering alternative to traditional Alfredo sauce: Cashew Crème Fraîche. With its velvety texture and rich flavor, this healthier version is sure to become a household favorite. Made with cashews and a few simple ingredients, it's easy to prepare and perfect for any pasta dish or even as a dip.

Ingredients

- 1 cup roasted unsalted or raw cashews, soaked overnight, drained
- 2 garlic cloves, minced
- 2 tablespoons nutritional yeast
- 1 tablespoon fresh lemon juice
- ¼ yellow onion, roughly chopped
- ¾ cup water
- ½ teaspoon Italian seasoning
- ¼ teaspoon rosemary
- ½ teaspoon thyme
- ½ teaspoon sea salt
- 1 (8-ounce) package Banza Penne Pasta
- **Garnish with fresh sliced or grated truffles, Nutty Parmesan, extra nutritional yeast, and fresh parsley or thyme**

Directions

In a high-speed blender or using the Twister Jar attachment for the Blendtec, blend the cashews, garlic, nutritional yeast, lemon juice, onion, water, Italian seasoning, rosemary, thyme, and sea salt until smooth and cream.

Meanwhile, cook the pasta according to package instructions. Once the pasta is cooked and drained, toss it with a portion of the Cashew Crème Fraîche and top with your favorite garnish. Store any remaining sauce in an airtight container in the fridge for up to 5 days.

Parmesan Polenta & Mushrooms

Yield: 2 servings

Ingredients

2 cups oat milk
1 cup polenta
Sea salt to taste
¼ cup shredded Parmesan cheese
½ teaspoon avocado oil
1 white onion, finely diced
½ red bell pepper, sliced
1 (16-ounce) package of your favorite mushrooms, sliced
2–3 tablespoons water or broth
2 tablespoons julienned sun-dried tomatoes in oil
1 tablespoon sun-dried tomato oil from jar
2 tablespoons Greek seasoning
Pinch of fresh thyme
Pepper to taste
Garnish with fresh thyme sprigs

Directions

Warm the oat milk in a saucepan over medium heat, stirring occasionally. Once it begins to bubble, whisk in the polenta and sea salt. Reduce the heat to a simmer and cook for 20 minutes, stirring occasionally, until the polenta reaches the desired texture. For a smoother, creamier texture, cook longer; for a grittier texture, cook less. Once cooked, gently fold in the Parmesan cheese until well combined.

While the polenta is cooking, heat the avocado oil in a skillet over medium heat. Sauté the onion for approximately 5 minutes, until it starts to caramelize. Add the red bell pepper and mushrooms, and cook for an additional 7–10 minutes until softened. Add 2–3 tablespoons of water or broth to deglaze the pan. Stir to loosen any browned bits and simmer for 1–2 minutes until it slightly reduces. Stir in the sun-dried tomatoes, oil, Greek seasoning, a pinch of fresh thyme, and pepper to taste. Cook for a few more minutes to blend the flavors.

To serve, ladle a portion of the polenta into individual bowls and generously top with the sautéed vegetables and the pan sauce, topped with fresh thyme sprigs.

Bold Border Sauce

Yield: 4 servings

Unlock the versatility of Bold Border Sauce, a dynamic addition to countless dishes. After whipping up a batch, explore imaginative ways to elevate your meals.

Ingredients

- 1 can black beans, drained and rinsed
- 1 can fire-roasted tomatoes
- 1 cup frozen organic corn
- 1 tablespoon fresh lime juice
- 1 tablespoon white balsamic vinegar
- 1 teaspoon Mexican Fiesta seasoning

Directions

Combine all ingredients into a saucepan and heat over medium for approximately 5 minutes, stirring occasionally to blend the flavors. Use immediately with your favorite dish. Any leftover can be stored in an airtight container in the fridge for up to 3 days.

Bold Border Quesadillas: Spread butter on a tortilla and place it butter-side down in a frying pan. Add a generous dollop of Bold Border Sauce and your favorite ingredients such as cilantro, jalapeños, Mexican-style cheese shreds, and red onion. Cook over medium heat until golden, then flip and repeat on the other side.

Bold Border Salad: Drizzle over your preferred mixed greens and top with sour cream, olives, red onions, diced bell pepper, jalapeños, cilantro, and Mexican-style cheese shreds.

Bold Border Burrito: Warm a tortilla; spread with Bold Border Sauce. Fill with Spanish rice, refried beans, Mexican-style cheese shreds, and cilantro. Roll it up and enjoy.

Bold Border Taco: Fill a warmed corn tortilla with a generous dollop of Bold Border Sauce. Top with jalapeños, sour cream, cilantro, red onions, and Mexican-style cheese shreds.

Bold Border Taco Salad with Tortilla Chips: Line a bowl with tortilla chip, then drizzle with Bold Border Sauce. Add your favorite toppings such as yellow or red bell peppers, sliced raw jalapeños, sour cream, chopped cilantro or parsley, and a squeeze of lime juice.

Rustic Cornbread Skillet

Yield: 8 slices

Ingredients for Filling

1 onion, diced
1 tablespoon avocado oil
1 bell pepper, diced
1 pound Beyond Beef Plant-Based Ground
½ jalapeño, seeded and finely chopped
1 cup organic frozen corn
3 garlic cloves, minced
2 teaspoons Mexican Fiesta seasoning
1½ teaspoons chili powder
½ teaspoon sea salt
Pepper to taste

Ingredients for Cornbread Topping

1 cup cornmeal
1 cup unbleached all-purpose flour by King Arthur Baking Company*
1 tablespoon baking powder
½ teaspoon sea salt
1 cup oat milk or soy milk
¼ cup olive oil
¼ cup maple syrup
Garnish with sour cream, fresh cilantro, and zesty salsa

Directions

Preheat your oven to 375°F. In a cast-iron skillet, sauté the onion in avocado oil over medium heat for about 3 minutes until it starts to soften. Add the bell pepper and Beyond Meat Plant-Based Ground Beef, breaking up the meat as it cooks. When the meat is nearly browned, stir in the jalapeño, corn, garlic, Mexican Fiesta seasoning, chili powder, sea salt, and pepper. Continue cooking for a few additional minutes, stirring occasionally. Remove the skillet from the heat and set it aside.

Continued…

For the cornbread topping, sift together the cornmeal, flour, baking powder, and sea salt in a mixing bowl. Add the oat milk, olive oil, and maple syrup, whisking until the batter is smooth. Pour the cornbread batter evenly over the vegetable filling in the skillet.

Bake uncovered for 25–30 minutes. Check for doneness by inserting a toothpick into the cornbread. If it comes out clean, it's ready. Once baked, remove from the oven and let it cool for a few minutes to set the cornbread. Garnish with sour cream, fresh cilantro, and zesty salsa.

Author's Note: While this recipe uses white flour, which can cause inflammation in some individuals, feel free to replace it with Bob's Red Mill Gluten Free 1-to-1 Baking Flour. However, the cornbread will come out a bit thinner and not as fluffy.

Feel free to experiment with different fillings to create your own unique version. For a lighter option, omit the meat and add more veggies such as chopped zucchini, broccoli, mushrooms, spinach, or any of your favorite vegetables. The versatility of this dish allows you to customize it to your taste and dietary preferences.

Carb-Free Pizza Bowl

Yield: 2 servings

Savor the taste of a loaded pizza without the crust with my Carb-Free Pizza Bowl. Enjoy all the flavorful toppings in every bite!

Ingredients
- 3 tablespoons avocado oil
- 1 red bell pepper, thin sliced
- 1 green bell pepper, thin sliced
- 2½-ounces pepperoni, sliced*
- ¼ cup fire-roasted canned tomatoes
- 2 tablespoons pizza seasoning
- 1 cup chopped spinach or arugula
- Garnish with your favorite pizza toppings

Directions

Heat avocado oil in a cast-iron skillet and sauté bell peppers for about 5 minutes, stirring occasionally until they begin to brown. Add pepperoni and continue to sauté until charred. Mix in the remaining ingredients, stirring gently, and simmer until the greens are just wilted. Divide the mixture between two bowls and top with your favorite pizza garnishes.

Transform your Carb-Free Pizza Bowl into a standout appetizer by mincing the ingredients and preparing them as directed. Serve with a bowl of tortilla chips for a unique party snack that combines the best of chips and pizza. Experiment with toppings such as pineapple, Beyond Meat Hot Italian Sausage, melted cheese, Parmesan, mozzarella, nutritional yeast, red pepper flakes, olives, and fresh basil. For something truly unique, add a dollop of pesto or Cashew Basil Blitz (page 173).

For additional serving ideas, try it over quinoa or wild rice, or swap fire-roasted tomatoes with sun-dried tomatoes in olive oil and add sliced cherry tomatoes. Let your creativity shine!

Author's Note: For a healthier homemade alternative, check out the Vegan Pepperoni recipe (page 250). Although this pepperoni contains gluten, it incorporates healthier ingredients overall.

Roasted Eggplant Tzatziki

Yield: 3–4 servings

Ingredients

1 large eggplant, sliced lengthwise (⅛ -inch pieces)
4–5 organic heirloom or vine ripened tomatoes, sliced
2 tablespoons avocado oil
¼ teaspoon sea salt
Pepper to taste
3–4 tortillas
3–4 tablespoons sunflower seeds
Garnish with fresh dill and Tzatziki Dip*

Directions

Preheat the oven to 400°F. Arrange the eggplant and tomatoes on a baking sheet. Drizzle with avocado oil and season with sea salt and pepper. Roast for 15 minutes, then switch to broil for an additional 4–5 minutes, or until the veggies are golden. Warm the tortillas while the vegetables roast.

To assemble, place a generous amount of roasted veggies on each tortilla. Sprinkle with sunflower seeds and garnish with fresh dill and Tzatziki Dip. Wrap and enjoy!

Author's Note: For a homemade option, refer to the Tzatziki Dip recipe (page 234), or for variety, try the Spicy Garlic Aioli (page 234). Store-bought alternatives such as Plant-Based Tzatziki Style Dip by Good Foods or Simple Truth Plant Based Cauliflower Dip Tzatziki are also excellent alternatives.

Boston Baked Lentils

Yield: 4 servings

Ingredients
1 cup dried lentils, soaked overnight, drained
3 cups water
½ teaspoon sea salt
1 tablespoon avocado oil
2 garlic cloves, minced
1 red bell pepper
¼ red onion, peeled, sliced
¼ teaspoon unsulfured molasses
¼ teaspoon maple syrup
¼ teaspoon smoked paprika
¼ teaspoons apple cider vinegar
4 TortillaLand uncooked tortillas
Garnish with roasted red pepper hummus and fresh thyme leaves

Directions

Rinse the lentils and add them to a large soup pot with 3 cups water. Bring to a boil, then reduce to a simmer and cook for 30–45 minutes until tender, adding sea salt about 5 minutes before they're done.

While the lentils cook, heat avocado oil in a skillet over medium heat. Sauté the garlic, red bell pepper, and red onion for 5 minutes, or until softened. Stir in the molasses, maple syrup, smoked paprika, and apple cider vinegar. Add 1 cup of cooked lentils to the skillet, mix well, and transfer to a serving dish.

Without washing the skillet, use it to heat tortillas for a minute or two on each side, letting them absorb the leftover flavors. Spread roasted red pepper hummus on each tortilla, add the Boston Baked Lentils, and sprinkle with fresh thyme. Fold the tortillas and serve.

Author's Note: TortillaLand uncooked tortillas contain wheat flour, which may not be suitable for those with intolerances. For a gluten-free option, use corn tortillas, chickpea grain-free tortillas, or those made from almond flour or cassava flour.

Leftover lentils can be refrigerated for later use. They make a great topping for salads, or can be used to fill quesadillas, tacos, or even a new variation of Golden Spice Puff Pockets (page 159). Get creative with your toppings by adding sautéed hot red chili peppers, sliced cherry tomatoes, or fresh greens.

Lemon Zoodles, Capers & Empress Tomatoes

Yield: 2 servings

Indulge in a fresh creation, carb-free, with arugula tossed in a delicate blend of lemon zest, capers, Empress tomatoes, and artichoke hearts!

Ingredients

1 small red onion, thinly sliced
2 tablespoons extra-virgin olive oil
3 small zucchinis, ends removed, spiralized
3–4 tablespoons lemon juice
2 tablespoons sun-dried tomatoes, packed in oil
2 tablespoons sun-dried tomato oil
16 Empress tomatoes, halved
4 artichoke hearts in oil
5 Greek olives and kalamata olives
1 handful arugula
Pepper to taste
Garnish with fresh basil and Nutty Parmesan

Directions

Sauté the red onion in olive oil over low heat for a couple of minutes. Add the spiralized zucchinis (zoodles) and cook for an additional 3 minutes, tossing occasionally. Add lemon juice, sun-dried tomatoes with their oil, and Empress tomatoes. Use a masher to gently smash the tomatoes during cooking to create a flavorful sauce. Cook for a couple more minutes before adding the artichoke hearts, olives, arugula, and pepper. You may not need to add additional salt, as the olives and Parmesan will provide enough seasoning. Gently toss everything together until well combined. Serve in two pasta bowls and top with fresh basil and Nutty Parmesan (page 233).

For additional variations, consider incorporating spinach and pizza seasoning.

Arugula Linguine with Lemon Zest & Capers

Yield: 2 servings

Ingredients

½ package of Banza Linguine Noodles (about 4 ounces)
¼ cup olive oil
4 tablespoons lemon juice
1 tablespoon capers
1 cup sliced grape tomatoes
2 cups chopped arugula
Sea salt and pepper to taste

Directions

Cook the linguine according to the package instructions until al dente. While the pasta cooks, combine olive oil, lemon juice, capers, tomatoes, arugula, sea salt, and pepper in a large bowl. Toss well and set aside. Once the linguine is cooked, drain it and add it to the bowl with the other ingredients. Gently toss everything together until the pasta is evenly coated. This dish is best enjoyed chilled. Pop it in the fridge for 30 minutes before serving.

For variations, consider adding marinated artichoke hearts, fresh spinach, sun-dried tomatoes, briny Greek olives, or a sprinkle of Nutty Parmesan (page 233).

Pasta alla Bella Capri

Yield: 2 servings

Ingredients

½ package of Banza Linguine Noodles (about 4 ounces)*
1 tablespoon rock salt, optional
2 tablespoons extra-virgin olive oil
¼ cup capers, rinsed
1 teaspoon red miso paste
5 garlic cloves, minced
¼ cup minced fresh parsley
1 (28-ounce) can crushed tomatoes
½ cup kalamata olives
Garnish with fresh parsley, red pepper flakes, and Nutty Parmesan (page 233)

Directions

Cook the linguine according to the package instructions until al dente, adding a pinch of rock salt, if desired. While the pasta cooks, heat olive oil over low heat in a skillet. Add the capers and cook gently, then stir in the red miso paste until it nearly dissolves. Add the minced garlic and simmer for a few minutes before adding fresh parsley and crushed tomatoes. Allow the sauce to simmer slowly to develop the flavors.

Meanwhile, squeeze the kalamata olives over the sauce, allowing the olives to break apart and letting their juices enrich the sauce. Continue simmering until the pasta is ready. Drain the pasta and toss it with the sauce. Serve garnished with fresh parsley, red pepper flakes, and Nutty Parmesan.

Author's Note: Feel free to use any pasta you prefer, such as penne or regular spaghetti. You can also replace the pasta with zoodles for a light, low-carb alternative.

For the perfect pairing, enjoy this dish with a glass of Chianti, Barbera, or a full-bodied Viognier, which complements the rich and aromatic flavors of this dish beautifully.

Peanut & Cashew Asian Stir-fry

Yield: 2 Servings

Ingredients

½ package udon noodles (about 4 ounces)*
1–2 tablespoons peanut oil
½ cup sliced celery, optional
1 small onion, thinly sliced
4 garlic cloves, minced
Sea salt to taste
1½ red bell pepper, thinly sliced
1 tablespoon shredded fresh ginger
½ block tofu, cubed, optional
¼ teaspoon red chili peppers or jalapeño pepper, minced, optional
1 small head of broccoli, florets removed and chopped
2 tablespoons tamari
2 tablespoons toasted sesame oil
1 handful spinach
Peanut Sauce (page 199)
Garnish with chopped cashews or peanuts, green onion, cilantro, lime juice, and hot chili oil

Directions

Prepare the udon noodles according to package instructions. In a skillet, heat the peanut oil over medium heat. Add the celery and onion, sautéing for about 3 minutes, stirring occasionally. Add the garlic, sea salt, bell pepper, ginger, tofu, and red chile peppers. Continue to sauté for an additional 5 minutes. Toss in the broccoli, tamari, and sesame oil, mixing well. Cover the skillet to steam the veggies for about 5 minutes, stirring occasionally until they reach your desired texture.

In the final minutes of cooking, add the spinach and a few tablespoons of Peanut Sauce (page 199). Mix well and cook until the spinach is slightly wilted. Divide the cooked udon noodles between two bowls and top with the stir-fry. Drizzle with the remaining Peanut Sauce and garnish with chopped nuts, green onion, cilantro, lime juice, and a few drops of hot chili oil for extra flavor.

Continued…

Author's Note: Udon noodles contain gluten, but you can use any base that suits your preferences. For a gluten-free option, consider soba noodles (ensure they are 100 percent buckwheat), saifun bean threads (made from mung beans), or vermicelli rice noodles. You can also serve the stir-fry over quinoa or wild rice. Select the base that best suits your preferences.

Replace the red chili peppers or jalapeño peppers with a dash of cayenne pepper or red pepper flakes for a similar spicy flavor. Feel free to garnish with fresh pineapple chunks or shredded carrots. Customize the stir-fry with vegetables of your choice, such as mushrooms, green beans, zucchini, or squash.

Peanut Sauce

Yield: 2 Servings

Ingredients

¼ cups light tamari

3 tablespoons peanut butter

2 tablespoons maple syrup

½ tablespoon white vinegar

1–2 teaspoons sesame oil

1 teaspoon organic sriracha by Sky Valley

2 garlic cloves, minced

½ teaspoon grated or minced ginger

¼ teaspoon Chinese five-spice powder

Directions

Whisk together tamari, peanut butter, maple syrup, white vinegar, sesame oil, sriracha, garlic, ginger, and Chinese five-spice powder in a small bowl. Set aside to enhance the flavor profile of your Peanut & Cashew Asian Stir-fry (page 196).

Spicy Moroccan Loaded Sweet Potato

Yield: 2 servings

Ingredients

2 sweet potatoes
2 tablespoons coconut oil, divided
1 red onion, sliced
1 small whole bulb garlic, cloves individually sliced
1 pound cremini mushrooms, sliced
3 handfuls spinach, chopped
2 tablespoons lemon juice
1 teaspoon maple syrup
2 tablespoons tamari
2 teaspoons smoked paprika
2 teaspoons cumin
Dash cayenne
Sea salt to taste, optional
Garnish with diced avocado, salsa, Cashew Crèma Mexicana, cilantro, and a squeeze of lemon juice if desired

Directions

Preheat your oven to 400°F. Slice each sweet potato lengthwise and drizzle with 1 tablespoon of coconut oil, adding a pinch of sea salt. Place them face down on a baking pan and roast for 30 minutes, or until they are fork-tender.

While the sweet potatoes roast, heat the remaining 1 tablespoon of coconut oil in a skillet over medium heat. Sauté the red onion and garlic for about 5 minutes, or until caramelized. Add the mushrooms and cook until they are golden brown. Once the mushrooms are cooked, add spinach, lemon juice, maple syrup, tamari, smoked paprika, cumin, cayenne, and a pinch of sea salt. Toss everything together until the spinach wilts slightly. Set aside.

Once the sweet potatoes are done roasting, plate them and use a fork to gently mash the inside, creating a bowl shape for the toppings. Spoon a bit of the sautéed mixture into each sweet potato half. Garnish with avocado, salsa, Cashew Crèma Mexicana (page 232), cilantro, and a squeeze of lemon juice if desired.

Sweet Indulgence

Savor the Magic in Every Bite

Edible Maple Almond Chocolate Chip Oat Cookie Dough

Yield: 2 servings

Ingredients

- 1 cup oats
- 1 cup almond flour
- ⅓ cup maple syrup
- ¼ teaspoon sea salt
- 1 tablespoon vanilla extract
- ⅓ cup chocolate chips

Directions

In a food processor, pulse the oats until they become mealy. Add the almond flour, maple syrup, sea salt, and vanilla, then blend until well combined. Gently fold in the chocolate chips by pulsing a few times to distribute them evenly. Scoop the dough using an ice cream scoop and transfer it to a bowl and enjoy.

For a smoother texture, grind the oats into flour before mixing with the other ingredients. For a quicker option, mix all the ingredients by hand in a bowl and shape them into balls or flatten into cookies. Alternatively, turn them into Maple Almond Chocolate Chip Oat Cookie Dough Pops (page 206).

Customize your dough by adding cinnamon, cacao powder, shredded coconut, or chopped nuts. For a café-inspired variety, add espresso powder and top with coconut whipped cream, cherries, and chopped peanuts. Experiment to find your perfect flavor combination.

Maple Almond Chocolate Chip Oat Cookie Dough Pops

Yield: 1–2 servings

Ingredients

 Edible Maple Almond Chocolate Chip Oat Cookie Dough (page 205)
 5.3-ounce cup plant-based vanilla yogurt*
 Silicone Popsicle mold*
 1–2 Popsicle sticks

Directions

Prepare the Edible Maple Almond Chocolate Chip Oat Cookie Dough recipe on the previous page, ensuring it is well-mixed. Add 1 (5.3-ounce) cup of plant-based vanilla yogurt to the cookie dough and blend until smooth. Spoon the mixture into the silicone Popsicle mold, and shake the mold gently to settle the ingredients and ensure even freezing. Insert a Popsicle stick into each mold and freeze overnight. Once chilled, remove the pops by pressing on the back; lifting from the stick may cause them to fall apart.

Author's Note: Silicone molds, such as the flat Lékué Large Stackable Popsicle Molds, are recommended for easy release and a good fit in the freezer.

This recipe is perfect to sink your teeth into and adds a cool refreshing treat on a hot summer day. For a more solid texture, use 2 cups of plant-based vanilla yogurt. These pops are a healthier alternative to traditional ice cream, with a delicious blend of maple, almond, and chocolate chip flavors.

Rocky Road Fudge

Yield: 6 servings

This healthier take on classic fudge is made with all-natural ingredients and is quick to prepare. Enjoy a spoonful straight from the bowl if you can't wait. Plus, raw cacao is rich in antioxidants and flavonoids that support heart health and elevate your mood.

Ingredients

¼ cup cocoa powder
¾ cup cacao powder
1 cup maple syrup
½ cup natural peanut butter
2 teaspoons vanilla extract
¾ teaspoon sea salt
¾ cup cacao butter, melted
Garnish with a handful of Dandies Vegan Marshmallows, salted almonds, or walnuts

Directions

In a high-speed blender, combine all ingredients, except the garnish, adding the melted cacao butter last. Blend until smooth and creamy. Pour the mixture into molds or a parchment paper-lined small casserole dish. Gently fold in your choice of marshmallows, almonds, or walnuts, ensuring they are evenly distributed. Refrigerate for 30 minutes to set. Once firm, remove the fudge from the molds, or, if using a casserole dish, cut into chunks. For longer storage, freeze in an airtight ziplock freezer bag for up to 3 weeks.

Experiment with different nut butters such as cashew, hazelnut, or almond for variety. Deepen the flavor with only 1 drop of almond or peppermint extract, but use these extracts sparingly due to their potency. Alternatively, replace the nuts and marshmallows with coconut flakes or top with freeze-dried strawberries for a burst of fruity goodness.

Cocoa Jungle Monkey Mousse

Yield: 3 servings

Dive into the creamy and decadent goodness of Cocoa Jungle Monkey Mousse, a sweet treat that's simple, easy, and healthy enough to enjoy for breakfast too!

Ingredients

- **2 large bananas, peeled**
- **½ cup coconut cream***
- **¼ cup cacao powder**
- **3 tablespoons maple syrup**

Directions

Combine all the ingredients in the Twister Jar attachment for the Blendtec or a high-speed blender; blend until smooth and creamy. Pour the mousse into three 4-ounce serving cups or two 6-ounce cups. Refrigerate for a few hours until set. The chilled mousse will be thick, rich, and creamy.

Author's Note: You may use 1 can organic coconut milk where the only ingredients are coconut, water, and guar gum. Each can contains approximately 1 cup coconut cream. Keep the can in the coldest part of the refrigerator until use. Do not shake the can or the cream and liquid will emulsify. We want to keep it separated. After opening, carefully scoop the cream from the top.

For an extra touch, garnish with So Delicious CocoWhip or nondairy Reddi-wip, shaved Choco Latte Rich & Bold Coffee Truffle Filled Oat Milk Chocolate by TCHO, or Luxurious Chocolate Masterpieces (page 216).

Cherry Sorbet

Yield: 2 servings

Ingredients for the Sorbet

1½ cups of frozen cherries or blueberries
¼ cup + 1 tablespoon coconut milk
2 tablespoons maple syrup

Directions

In the Twister Jar attachment for the Blendtec or a high-speed blender, combine the frozen berries, coconut milk, and maple syrup. Pulse the mixture for a few seconds at a time until it reaches a smooth, creamy consistency. Serve immediately and enjoy.

For a Chunky Cherry Chocolate Sorbet, add 2 tablespoons of dried tart cherries and 2 chunks of Choco Latte Rich & Bold Coffee Truffle Filled Oat Milk Chocolate during the last part of the blending process.

With each spoonful, savor the chewy sweetness of the cherries and the decadent coffee notes of the Choco Latté Truffles. As pictured, this sorbet features a mix of cherry and blueberry. Feel free to experiment with different frozen fruits to create your own version of this irresistible sorbet.

Truffle Joy Bombs

Yield: 2 servings, 6 truffles

Ingredients
- 1 cup almond flour
- ¼ cup cacao powder
- ¼ cup coconut oil, melted
- ¼ cup maple syrup
- 1 teaspoon vanilla extract
- Pinch of sea salt

Directions

In a small bowl, combine almond flour and cacao powder, mixing well. Add the melted coconut oil, maple syrup, vanilla, and a pinch of sea salt to the dry ingredients, stirring until a doughlike consistency forms. Cover the mixture and refrigerate for at least 30 minutes to set.

Once chilled, use a small ice cream scooper to portion out the mixture, then roll it into balls using your hands. For added flavor and texture, roll them in your choice of cacao powder, shredded coconut, freeze-dried strawberry powder, crushed nuts, or cocoa nibs.

For a nougaty twist reminiscent of Raisinets, add chopped raisins into the mixture before stirring. Enjoy these delicious Truffle Joy Bombs as a perfect bite-size treat!

Luxurious Chocolate Masterpieces

Yield: 6 servings

Meticulously crafted with raw cacao, these treats are rich in antioxidants, versatile, and satisfying. They're the perfect indulgence for any occasion, satisfying your sweet tooth and uplifting your mood. For foolproof chocolate, ensure precision in measurements.

Ingredients

½ cup melted cacao butter
1/2 cups cacao powder
¼ cup + 1 tablespoon maple syrup
2 teaspoons vanilla extract
Pinch of sea salt
2 teaspoons each peanut butter and jelly, optional
Silicone candy molds (shaped like peanut butter cups)

Directions

Melt the cacao butter in a small saucepan over low heat. Measure again to ensure you have exactly ½ cup melted cacao butter, adjusting by adding or removing any excess as needed. Once melted, remove from the heat and whisk in the cacao powder, maple syrup, vanilla, and sea salt until smooth.

Transfer the melted chocolate to a Pyrex measuring cup for easy pouring. Pour a thin layer of the chocolate into the bottom of each mold. Add peanut butter and swirls of jelly on top, then pour the remaining chocolate over them. Gently jiggle the mold to settle the ingredients and refrigerate for 1 hour until set.

Once chilled, remove from the molds and enjoy on their own or atop the Messy Loaded Almond Yogurt & Banana Nut Crunch (page 73) recipe or in the Chunky Cherry Chocolate Sorbet (page 213).

Each cup is a canvas, granting you the freedom to experiment with an array of unique fillings, such as chopped dried cherries, coconut flakes, chopped walnuts, and small Dandies Vegan Marshmallows. To create six square chocolate masterpieces, consider using a 2 × 2 × 1-inch silicone baking mold, ensuring all the goodies fit inside perfectly. Enjoy the creative process and savor the delicious results!

Ideas to spark your taste buds:

Surf's-Up Coconut: Add macaroon coconut and creamy peanut butter together for a tropical blend.

Chunky Nougat: Intertwine crunchy peanut pieces with the natural sweetness of sliced dates and/or raisins.

Classic Candy-Inspired Chocolate Bars: Replace the peanut butter and jelly with a decadent drizzle of Salted Caramel Fondue (page 219) to bring back memories of Rolos. For a nostalgic alternative to a Snickers bar, consider adding chopped nuts with the Salted Caramel Fondue.

Sweet Indulgence

Salted Caramel Fondue

Yield: Variable servings

This delicious Salted Caramel Fondue is perfect for drizzling over your Luxurious Chocolate Masterpieces (page 216), crisp sliced apples, ice cream, Ultimate Tsunami Cacao (page 229), and more. Once refrigerated, it solidifies, transforming it into Caramel Soft Chews to savor.

Ingredients

- ½ cup coconut oil, melted
- ⅓ cup peanut butter, cashew butter, or almond butter
- ½ cup maple syrup
- 1 teaspoon vanilla extract
- ¼ teaspoon sea salt

Directions

In a small saucepan over low heat, gently warm and whisk together all the ingredients for several minutes until creamy, resulting in a luscious, gooey caramel texture. Pour over your favorite treats and enjoy.

Feel free to add a dash of cinnamon or cardamom for an extra flavor boost. Let your creativity flow and indulge in the decadence!

Salted Caramel Chews

Directions

After creating the Salted Caramel Fondue (page 219), pour the sauce into silicone molds, adding nuts if desired, then refrigerate for 1 hour to create delicious Caramel Soft Chews. It's as easy as that! For an even simpler method, combine all of the Salted Caramel Fondue ingredients into a high-speed blender, blend until creamy, pour into molds, and refrigerate.

These chews are perfect for a quick, sweet snack or a delicious addition to your dessert platter. Experiment with different molds and nut additions to create your own unique treats.

Chocolate Bananasicles

Yield: Variable servings

If you have any surplus chocolate sauce after making this recipe, pour it into silicone molds and refrigerate for Luxurious Chocolate Masterpieces. Alternatively, store the excess in a sealed container in the fridge. When needed, melt it in a small saucepan over low heat and drizzle over pancakes or ice cream, or use it for chocolate dipped strawberries or a delectable fondue.

Ingredients

- **Luxurious Chocolate Masterpieces chocolate sauce (page 216)**
- **Popsicle sticks**
- **Bunch of ripe bananas**
- **Garnish with your choice of chopped peanuts, chopped honey pecan pieces, sprinkles, coconut, and more**

Directions

Create these irresistible treats by first making the chocolate sauce from the Luxurious Chocolate Masterpieces recipe (page 216). Once ready, pour the sauce into a narrow mug or glass. Insert Popsicle sticks into the bananas and dip them into the melted chocolate. Lay them on a parchment paper–lined tray and sprinkle with your favorite toppings such as chopped nuts or coconut. Freeze until the chocolate sets. These are perfect for summer parties or as a year-round indulgence.

Fun Orange Treats

Yield: 2 servings

Recipe inspired by Jen from Lean Bellas Kitchen

This fun and simple recipe is perfect for making with kids, using just three ingredients. You might want to double the recipe because these treats are so irresistible, and you can enjoy them guilt-free.

Ingredients

- **1 cup mandarin orange juice, approx. 4–5 oranges**
- **1 teaspoon agar powder**
- **1–2 tablespoons honey or your preferred sweetener**
- **Silicone molds**

Directions

Heat the mandarin orange juice in a saucepan over medium heat. Stir in the agar powder and sweetener until the agar is completely dissolved. Allow the mixture to simmer for about 1 minute, then remove from the heat. Pour the mixture into your chosen molds and refrigerate for an hour, or until fully set.

Author's Note: Agar, a gelatinous substance derived from algae, is a vegetarian-friendly alternative to traditional gelatin. It is tasteless, odorless, and rich in dietary fiber, making it ideal for a variety of desserts and culinary creations.

For a creative touch, consider adding small fruit pieces like strawberries or blueberries to the molds before pouring in the mixture. This will enhance both the color and texture of your treats. Alternatively, pour the mixture into mandarin orange halves for a fun, natural presentation that adds a vibrant touch.

Golden Milk

Yield: 1 serving

Ingredients

   1 cup coconut or preferred plant-based milk
   2 teaspoons Turmeric Golden Paste (page 42)

Directions

Warm the coconut milk and Turmeric Golden Paste in a saucepan until it reaches your preferred temperature. Pour the Golden Milk into a mug and sip slowly in the evening to promote a restful night's sleep.

Reishi Mushroom Turmeric Latte

Yield: 1 serving

Indulge in the soothing warmth of a Reishi Mushroom Turmeric Latte, perfect for winding down your day and promoting restful sleep.

Ingredients
　　1 cup coconut milk
　　1 cinnamon stick
　　1 whole star anise pod
　　1-inch piece fresh ginger root, chopped or minced
　　½ teaspoon turmeric powder
　　½ teaspoon reishi mushroom powder
　　Pinch of black pepper
　　Garnish with a dash of cinnamon and cayenne

Directions

In a small saucepan, combine all ingredients and bring to a boil. Reduce heat and let simmer for 20 minutes. Strain the liquid through a cheesecloth into a mug and sip slowly. For a creative touch, sprinkle a dash of cinnamon and cayenne pepper on top before serving. Sip slowly and enjoy.

Author's Note: Store the strained cinnamon stick, anise, and ginger in an airtight container in the fridge for a few days, as they can be reused for up to 3 servings.

Ultimate Tsunami Cacao

Yield: 2 servings

Before you begin, note that the basic recipe is rated one spoon for simplicity. However, if you would like the Ultimate Tsunami Cacao experience, the difficulty rating increases to three spoons. Read through the entire recipe to gather all the toppings you'd like to use, such as the homemade Salted Caramel Fondue (page 219) or shaved Luxurious Chocolate Masterpieces (page 216). This will ensure you have everything ready for the ultimate experience.

Ingredients

- 1½ cups oat milk
- ½ teaspoon Bourbon Pecan Coffee by The Lawman Rub Co., optional
- 2 tablespoons cacao powder
- 2 tablespoons maple syrup
- 2 tablespoons Lily's dark chocolate chips
- ¼ teaspoon vanilla extract
- ⅛ teaspoon cinnamon
- Pinch of sea salt
- Garnish ideas below

Directions

Warm the oat milk in a small saucepan over medium-low heat until it begins to steam. Whisk in the Bourbon Pecan Coffee (if using), cacao powder, maple syrup, chocolate chips, vanilla, cinnamon, and a pinch of sea salt until smooth. Continue to cook for 3–5 minutes, stirring occasionally. Pour into one large mug or two smaller ones, if sharing, and garnish.

Now the fun begins! Turn your hot cacao into the Ultimate Tsunami by topping it with lots of goodies, such as Dandies Vegan Marshmallows, whipped coconut cream, or nondairy Reddi-wip. Drizzle with homemade Salted Caramel Fondue (page 219), sprinkle with cinnamon, and add shaved Luxurious Chocolate Masterpieces (page 216). If you haven't made the chocolate masterpieces yet, fear not! Opt for the delectable Choco Latte Rich & Bold Coffee Truffle Filled Oat Milk Chocolate as a fantastic alternative. For an extra kick, consider adding a dash of cayenne to spice things up.

Sweet Indulgence

Special Artisan Creations

Crafted Flavors for the Discerning Palate

Cashew Crèma Mexicana

Yield: 14 ounces

Ingredients

    1 cup raw cashews
    ¾ cup water, divided
    2 tablespoons lime juice
    1 tablespoon apple cider vinegar
    ½ teaspoon sea salt
    1 tablespoon nutritional yeast

Directions

Boil the cashews in a pot filled with water for 5 minutes, then drain. In a high-speed blender or using the Twister Jar attachment for the Blendtec, blend the cashews with ½ cup of water, lime juice, apple cider vinegar, sea salt, and nutritional yeast. If a thinner consistency is desired, gradually add more water, but do not exceed a total of ¾ cup. Use immediately or store in the fridge in an airtight container for up to 4–5 days.

Enhance your crèma by adding ½ teaspoon of Mexican oregano, ½ teaspoon of garlic powder, and ½ teaspoon of onion powder. Feel free to explore other flavor enhancements to suit your taste. Excellent additions might include ¼ teaspoon of smoked paprika, 1 tablespoon of fresh cilantro, or a dash of chili powder.

Nutty Parmesan

Yield: 10 ounces

Ingredients

- 1 cup unsalted raw cashews
- 3 tablespoons nutritional yeast
- 2 teaspoons apple cider vinegar powder
- 1 teaspoon sea salt

Directions

In a food processor, pulsate the unsalted raw cashews until they reach the desired consistency of Parmesan. Add the nutritional yeast, apple cider vinegar powder, and sea salt. Pulse the mixture again until thoroughly blended. Store in an airtight container in the fridge for up to a month until ready to use.

This Parmesan is versatile to your taste preferences. Feel free to add 1 teaspoon of garlic powder or any herbs you desire to enhance the flavor. Enjoy this delicious and healthy alternative to traditional Parmesan, perfect for sprinkling on pastas, salads, and more!

Spicy Garlic Aioli

Yield: 4 ounces

Looking for a healthier alternative to traditional mayonnaise? Give my Spicy Garlic Aioli a try. It's dairy-free, oil-free, sugar-free, and perfect for burgers, veggie dips, burritos, or even just licking off a spoon!

Ingredients

- ½ cup cashews, presoaked
- 2 small garlic cloves
- 3 tablespoons lemon juice
- 1 tablespoon organic raw coconut vinegar or apple cider vinegar
- ¼ cup water
- ½ teaspoon mustard powder
- ¼ teaspoon sea salt
- ½ teaspoon tzatziki seasoning

Directions

Presoak cashews overnight, then drain. Place the cashews into the Twister Jar attachment for the Blendtec or a high-speed blender along with all the other ingredients. Blend until smooth. Pour the mixture into a 4-ounce mason jar, seal, and refrigerate. Enjoy this delicious and healthy spread anytime you need it.

Tzatziki Dip anyone? This versatile recipe can easily be transformed into tzatziki. Simply omit the mustard powder and increase the tzatziki seasoning by an additional 1 teaspoon. Add a 3-inch length of diced English cucumber and 2 tablespoons of chopped fresh dill. Blend until smooth and creamy, then stir in an additional 3-inch piece of diced cucumber for texture. Enjoy drizzling it on your favorite dishes!

Chipotle Sauce

Yield: approx. 1 cup

Ingredients

⅓ cup raw cashews, presoaked
1 Anaheim pepper*
½ cup water
1 small garlic clove
2 teaspoons lime juice
½ teaspoon chipotle seasoning
Pinch of sea salt

Directions

Presoak cashews overnight, then drain. Broil the Anaheim pepper on a baking sheet until its skin is evenly charred, turning it few times. Allow the pepper to cool slightly, then carefully remove the charred skin, stem, and seeds.

Combine the peeled pepper, cashews, water, garlic clove, lime juice, chipotle seasoning, and sea salt in the Twister Jar attachment for the Blendtec or a high-speed blender. Blend until smooth and creamy. Pour the sauce into a 4-ounce mason jar, seal, and refrigerate. Enjoy this delicious and healthy spread anytime you need it.

Author's Note: Anaheim can be replaced with any pepper of your choice: poblano, red bell pepper, or red jalapeños.

Pico de Gallo

Yield: 2 cups

Recipe inspired by Jeannie Gagney

Ingredients

8 Roma tomatoes, diced
4 garlic cloves, minced
1 jalapeño, seeded and chopped*
½ medium red onion, diced
1 tablespoon chopped fresh cilantro leaves
2 tablespoons extra-virgin olive oil
½ teaspoon sea salt, or to taste
Black pepper to taste

Directions

In a medium bowl, combine the diced tomatoes, minced garlic, chopped jalapeño, diced red onion, and fresh cilantro. Drizzle with extra-virgin olive oil and season with sea salt and black pepper. Stir well to combine and refrigerate for a couple of hours to allow the flavors to meld. Before serving, strain any excess liquid to achieve the desired consistency.

Author's Note: This recipe is delicious atop the Cheesy Jalapeño Pop'n Breakfast Cups (page 71), Easy Skillet Breakfast Potatoes (page 72), or Rustic Cornbread Skillet (page 185), and also great on tacos, a dip for chips, a dollop inside an avocado half for a healthy snack, or as a topping for a Southwestern-style salad.

Love the vibrant flavors of pico de gallo but not a fan of the heat? Replace the jalapeño with red pepper flakes to taste. Feel free to get creative by substituting ingredients, add mango or corn (as pictured), or use your favorite peppers such as red jalapeños for a sweeter heat, serranos for an intense heat, or bell peppers for a milder option. Customize it to suit your taste.

Maple-Smoked Plant Ribbons

Yield: 8–10 rice papers

Ingredients

½ cup reduced-sodium tamari or coconut aminos
½ teaspoon liquid smoke
¼ cup maple syrup
1 teaspoon smoked paprika
Cracked pepper to taste
1 tablespoon nutritional yeast, optional
Water to thin flavor, if desired
8–10 rice papers

Directions

In a small bowl, whisk the tamari or coconut aminos, liquid smoke, maple syrup, paprika, cracked pepper, and nutritional yeast. Taste the mixture and add water if the flavor is too strong, as it will intensify when baked. Pour the liquid into a large round bowl, such as a pie pan. Submerge one rice paper at a time in the liquid, allowing it to soak for about 30 seconds. Place the soaked rice paper onto a cutting board and repeat with the remaining rice papers.

Stack 3–4 soaked rice papers on top of each other and use a sharp knife to cut thin slices. Lay the slices in a single layer on a parchment paper–lined toaster oven sheet. Avoid stacking multiple layers as they will not crisp up; stacked layers will be chewy rather than crunchy. Bake the rice paper slices in your toaster oven at 375°F for 5 minutes, keeping a watchful eye on them as they cook quickly. If using a conventional oven, the cook time may increase to 7–10 minutes total. Enjoy immediately or use as a topping for salads, soups, sandwiches, or wraps.

Eggplant Bacon

Yield: 6+ servings

Recipe inspired by Sarah Bond, CEO of Live Eat Learn

Ingredients

½ eggplant
1 tablespoon tamari
1 tablespoon olive oil
1 tablespoon maple syrup
1 teaspoon smoked paprika
½ teaspoon each salt, pepper, garlic powder, cumin
1 teaspoon vegan Worcestershire sauce

Directions

Preheat your oven or air fryer to 250°F. Slice the eggplant lengthwise into quarters, then cut into long strips about ⅛ inch thick to resemble bacon. Using a mandoline slicer ensures uniformity.

In a small bowl, combine tamari, olive oil, maple syrup, smoked paprika, salt, pepper, garlic powder, cumin, and vegan Worcestershire sauce. Brush this mixture generously on both sides of the eggplant strips.

For air frying, arrange the slices in a single layer and cook for 10–15 minutes until they are browned. For baking, place the slices on a parchment paper–lined baking sheet in a single layer and bake for 30–45 minutes, flipping halfway through to ensure even cooking.

Let the eggplant bacon cool slightly; it will continue to crisp up as it cools, achieving the ideal bacon-like crunch.

Prosecco Pickled Jalapeños

Yield: 16 ounces

Ingredients

    8 jalapeños, sliced
    8 garlic cloves
    6 fresh dill sprigs
    1 teaspoon sea salt
    1 tablespoon maple syrup
    ½ cup water
    ½ cup prosecco wine vinegar*

Directions

Layer the sliced jalapeños, garlic cloves, and dill sprigs in a 16-ounce mason jar; set aside. In a small saucepan, combine the sea salt, maple syrup, water, and prosecco wine vinegar. Bring to a boil, stirring constantly, and cook for 2 minutes. Carefully pour the hot mixture over the jalapeños in the mason jar, filling it to the brim. Seal the jar and let it cool on the countertop before refrigerating.

These zesty pickled jalapeños are a fantastic addition to pizzas, sandwiches, salads, macaroni salad, and more!

Love pickles? Swap the jalapeños for sliced mini cucumbers and use pickling spices instead to make Prosecco Pickles—just follow the same recipe and instructions!

Author's Note: Prosecco wine vinegar imparts a unique, refined flavor to these pickled jalapeños. If you enjoy the tangy bite of pickled vegetables, you can easily adapt this recipe to pickle other veggies, such as beets, carrots, celery, or okra. Can't find prosecco wine vinegar? You can use regular white distilled vinegar.

Pickled Tofu Feta

Yield: 8 ounces

Ingredients
½–¾ block organic firm tofu
1/2 teaspoon thyme
½ teaspoon oregano
Handful Castelvetrano olives, optional
½ cup water
⅓ cup white vinegar
1 tablespoon sea salt

Directions

Drain the tofu and pat it dry with a paper towel. Wrap the tofu in a clean dish towel and press it between heavy plates on a cutting board for 1–2 hours to remove excess moisture. Once pressed, cut the tofu into small cubes and place in a 16-ounce mason jar with the herbs (and the olives, if using).

In a small saucepan, heat the water, white vinegar, and sea salt until boiling. Pour the hot mixture over the tofu, ensuring it is fully submerged. Seal the jar and let it cool on the countertop. Once cooled, refrigerate overnight. The Pickled Tofu Feta will keep for up to 4 weeks in the refrigerator.

Enjoy this versatile tofu feta on its own or with toasted pita—be sure to use a bit of the flavorful marinade, too. It's perfect for adding to salads, wraps, Cali Almond Flour Crackers (page 101), sandwiches, or burgers. Feel free to adjust the herbs or add extras like fresh red Thai chili peppers, pickling spices, or olive brine to suit your taste!

Occasional Indulgences

Guilty Pleasures for Special Moments

This chapter is your invitation to savor some indulgent treats that may stray from the anti-inflammatory focus. While these recipes may contain ingredients such as sugar or white flour, they deserve a place in your kitchen for those special occasions when a little decadence is just what you need. So go ahead, treat yourself, and savor the goodness when the moment calls.

Fit Fritz Avocado Margarita

Yield: 20-ounce serving

Recipe inspired by Carrie Fritz

Ingredients

Lime wedge
Hibiscus salt
4 ounces tequila*
2 ounces orange liqueur*
1 ounce agave
2 ounces lime juice
1 avocado
2 cups ice

Directions

Moisten the rim of your glass with a lime wedge, then dip it into hibiscus salt to coat. In a blender, combine the tequila, orange liqueur, agave syrup, lime juice, avocado, and ice. Blend until smooth. Pour the margarita into the prepared glass and enjoy.

Author's Note: Alcohol may trigger inflammation in some individuals. Pay attention to how your body responds and use your best judgment to determine what works best for you.

For spicy kick, add jalapeño slices to the blender. To elevate the flavor, float a splash of Grand Marnier on top. This refreshing avocado margarita can be made a day in advance. However, it is not recommended to refrigerate it for more than a day as it will oxidize and lose its pleasant taste. Any leftovers can be frozen for a few weeks for future enjoyment.

Neapolitan-Style Pizza

Yield: 2 servings

This homemade pizza recipe has quickly become a family favorite, often surpassing our trips to the local pizzeria. Although it takes some time, the anticipation of the dough rising adds to the enjoyment. Plus, it's a cost-effective option compared to store-bought pizzas, and the taste is amazing!

Ingredients

- 1 cup 00 pizza flour
- 1 cup unbleached all-purpose flour by King Arthur Baking Company*
- ½ teaspoon active dry yeast
- 1 teaspoon sea salt
- ¾ cup water
- ½ teaspoon extra-virgin olive oil
- Garnish: 2 tablespoons Rao's Arrabbiata Sauce per pizza, Ricotta Balls (page 128), a dash of pizza seasoning, and your other desired toppings

Directions

In a food processor, combine the 00 flour, all-purpose flour, active dry yeast, and sea salt. Add water and pulse a few times, then process on low for 30 seconds until the mixture forms a ball. This method eliminates the need for kneading and makes cleanup a breeze. Shape the dough into a ball, coat it lightly with olive oil, and place it in a bowl. Cover tightly with plastic wrap and let it rise for 2 hours.

Once the dough has risen, divide it into four equal parts. Form each piece into a ball and place each in a separate airtight container to prevent drying out. Refrigerate overnight or for up to 3 days.

When ready to bake, take one piece of dough (enough for 1 person). Press down in the center to create raised edges. Flip the dough and gently stretch it with your fists into a circular motion. For a daring touch, toss it in the air while spinning. If using a rolling pin, the pizza will be thin and won't rise much while baking.

Remove the toaster oven rack and place it on a cutting board. Preheat your toaster oven to broil. Yes, keep the rack out for now. Place the shaped dough onto the rack, ensuring any drippings will be easy to clean. Layer your sauce, cheese, and any other preferred toppings onto the dough.

When the oven is preheated, slide the rack into the toaster oven using oven mitts. Set the timer for 10 minutes. At the 3- to 5-minute mark, rotate the rack or use a metal spatula to turn the pizza for even cooking. The pizza should be done in 10–12 minutes, depending on your toaster oven.

Top with extra pizza seasoning, if desired, and serve with red pepper flakes and spicy Rao's Arrabbiata Sauce for dipping. Enjoy your delicious homemade Neapolitan-style pizza!

Author's Note: While this recipe uses white flour, which can cause inflammation in some individuals, pay attention to how your body responds and use your best judgment to determine what works best for you.

Get creative! Load up on veggies or make a meat lover's pizza with plant-based alternatives, such as Beyond Beef Crumbles and soyrizo. For a plant-based pepperoni, check out the Vegan Pepperoni (page 250). My favorite combination is pineapple chunks and Prosecco Pickled Jalapeños (page 242). And for the sauce, consider swapping out Rao's Arrabbiata Sauce for a batch of homemade Giovanni's Spaghetti Sauce (page 170) to take your pizza to the next level.

Did I hear pizza party? Use the Stoke Pizza Oven for an authentic experience (as pictured). Preheat it to 750°F, use the whole dough instead of dividing it, and cook for 2 minutes, rotating every 20 seconds for an even, crispy crust. Be sure to sprinkle flour or cornmeal on the oven peel for easy sliding.

Vegan Pepperoni

Yield: 6 servings

Recipe inspired by Sarah Bond, CEO of Live Eat Learn

Ingredients

- 1½ cups vital wheat gluten
- ½ cup water
- ¼ cup tamari
- ¼ cup coconut oil (should be solid)*
- 2 teaspoons each crushed red pepper flakes, ground mustard seed, smoked paprika, garlic powder
- 1 teaspoon fennel seeds, crushed or roughly chopped
- 1 teaspoon liquid smoke

Directions

Combine all ingredients in a large bowl, stirring until a ball forms. Transfer the dough to a clean surface and knead for about 5 minutes, until the dough becomes elastic and cohesive. The dough may still be lumpy, which is okay. Divide the dough into two equal pieces and shape each into a log about 1 inch thick. Wrap each log tightly in aluminum foil, ensuring the foil overlaps to prevent opening during cooking, and twist the ends to secure.

Bring a pot of water to a boil with a steamer basket in place, then add the wrapped pepperoni logs to the basket. Cover and steam for 45 minutes, monitoring the water level to ensure it does not evaporate completely. After steaming, remove the logs from the basket and carefully unwrap them. Transfer the logs to the refrigerator to cool completely. Once chilled, use a sharp knife to slice each log into thin pepperoni slices. These slices can be used as you would traditional pepperoni, on pizza, sandwiches, Popcorn Paradise (page 95), Carb-Free Pizza Bowl (page 187), or crackers.

Author's Note: Solid coconut oil is essential for achieving the right texture. If your coconut oil is not solid, place it in the refrigerator until solid.

Easy Flour Tortillas

Yield: 8–12 tortillas

For best results, use a tortilla press to evenly flatten the dough, helping it puff up perfectly when cooked.

Ingredients

- 2 cups unbleached all-purpose flour by King Arthur Baking Company*
- ½ teaspoon sea salt
- 3 tablespoons extra-virgin olive oil
- ¾ cup warm water

Directions

In a large bowl, combine the flour and sea salt. Stir in the olive oil until the mixture resembles coarse crumbs. Gradually add the warm water, mixing until the dough comes together. Transfer the dough to a floured surface and knead for about 5 minutes, until smooth. Cover the dough with a damp cloth and let it rest for 15 minutes.

Divide the dough into 8–12 balls. Use a tortilla press to flatten each ball into a thin circle.

Moisture, compression, and heat are essential for perfect tortillas. A tortilla press helps achieve uniformly thin tortillas. As the tortillas cook, the moisture inside turns to steam and causes them to puff up. This puffing ensures even cooking throughout while preserving the right moisture and elasticity.

Heat a dry nonstick skillet over medium-high heat. Cook each tortilla for about 20 seconds on each side. Use a spatula to press the outer edge, encouraging the tortilla to puff. Continue cooking for 1½ to 2 minutes per side, flipping when bubbles appear. The tortillas should be lightly browned. Keep the cooked tortillas warm in a towel until ready to serve.

Dough balls can be stored in the fridge for up to 3 days. When ready to make fresh tortillas, let the dough balls come to room temperature before rolling them out.

Author's Note: This recipe uses white flour, which may cause inflammation in some individuals. Pay attention to how your body responds and use your best judgment to determine what works best for you.

Dutch Oven Cheesy Jalapeño Artisan Bread

Yield: 6+ servings

This easy recipe yields a warm, golden-brown artisan loaf packed with zesty pickled jalapeños and gooey cheese. It's a flavorful and cost-effective alternative to store-bought bread, perfect for enjoying fresh from the oven or alongside your favorite dishes.

Ingredients

1½ cups water

1 tablespoon active dry yeast

1 teaspoon maple syrup or sugar

3 cups unbleached all-purpose flour by King Arthur Baking Company + more for dusting*

1 teaspoon sea salt

1 tablespoon olive oil

½ cup shredded cheese

6 pickled jalapeños, sliced*

Directions

Warm the water to 110°F in a Pyrex measuring glass, which usually takes 45 seconds to 1 minute in the microwave. Add the yeast and maple syrup or sugar to the warm water, and let it sit for 5 minutes to activate. In a large glass bowl, combine the flour and sea salt.

Once the yeast is activated, pour it over the flour mixture and stir gently with a wooden spoon or silicone whisk until combined. Transfer the dough to a lightly floured surface and shape it into a ball. Lightly coat the dough with olive oil, return it to the bowl, and cover tightly with plastic wrap. For a quicker rise, place the bowl on an oven mitt or towel to keep the bottom warm. Cover with a towel and let the dough rise for 3–5 hours or overnight.

Preheat your Dutch oven to 450°F. Turn the risen dough onto a lightly floured surface, shape it into a ball, and flatten it slightly. Fold the dough a few times, then add the shredded cheese and jalapeños. Fold the dough again to encase the cheese and jalapeños.

Continued . . .

Place the shaped dough on parchment paper and carefully transfer it into the preheated Dutch oven. Cover and bake for 30 minutes. Uncover and continue baking for another 20-30 minutes, or until the crust is as crispy as you like. Keep an eye on it, as ovens vary.

When the bread reaches a golden, crunchy exterior, remove it from the oven and let it cool on a rack for 20 minutes. Enjoy your homemade creation!

Author's Note: This recipe uses white flour, which may cause inflammation in some individuals. Pay attention to how your body responds and use your best judgment to determine what works best for you. When choosing jalapeños, check the ingredient list for additives like calcium chloride. For a healthier option with a great crunch, use organic jalapeños with minimal ingredients or make your own. You can find the Prosecco Pickled Jalapeños recipe on page 242.

Infuse your Cheesy Jalapeño Artisan Bread with your own unique blends or delve into creative possibilities with the flavorful ideas suggested below.

Festive Harvest: Add candied pecans, dried cranberries, a hint of cinnamon, and a sprinkle of brown sugar. Brush the outer crust with maple glaze and top with a few pecans during the last minutes of baking for a sweet, festive touch.

European Bistro: Mix in fresh thyme leaves and grated Parmesan for a European flair. Perfect with butter.

Strawberry Fields Forever Donuts

Yield: 11–12 servings

Discover the sweet world of donuts crafted with aquafaba and a hint of lemon juice, creating a perfect blend of fluffy and crunchy textures complemented by a refreshing citrus zing. Though they do contain sugar, these donuts are perfect for special occasions or a memorable date night.

Ingredients for Donuts

¼ cup coconut oil, melted + more for greasing silicone molds
1 cup unbleached all-purpose flour by King Arthur Baking Company*
¾ cup almond flour
¼ cup granulated sugar*
2 teaspoons baking powder
1 teaspoon baking soda
¼ teaspoon sea salt
¾ cup aquafaba (liquid from canned chickpeas)
3 teaspoons lemon juice
2 teaspoons apple cider vinegar
2 teaspoons vanilla extract
¼ cup maple syrup
1 tablespoon lemon or lime zest
¼ cup oat milk
2 teaspoons SweetLeaf Sweet Drops Berry Liquid Stevia Sweetener, or strawberry flavor

Ingredients for Glaze

1 cup powdered sugar
3 tablespoons strawberry powder
½ teaspoon SweetLeaf Sweet Drops Berry Liquid Stevia Sweetener
3 tablespoons plant-based milk
Garnish with coconut flakes, dried rose petals, or edible flowers.

Continued...

Directions

Preheat your oven to 375°F and grease a 12-count silicone donut mold with coconut oil. In a bowl, sift and whisk together the flour, almond flour, sugar, baking powder, baking soda, and sea salt.

In a separate bowl, combine the aquafaba and lemon juice, then whip with electric mixer until frothy soft peaks form. Add the ¼ cup coconut oil, apple cider vinegar, vanilla, maple syrup, lemon zest, oat milk, and berry stevia to the whipped aquafaba. Briefly whisk to combine, then gently fold the mixture into the dry ingredients until just blended.

Transfer the batter to a piping bag and fill the greased donut molds, ensuring not to overfill as they will rise. Bake at 375°F for 28 minutes until golden and a toothpick inserted into the center comes out clean. Let them cool in the molds for a few minutes, then transfer them to a wire rack to cool completely before glazing. To transfer, place the rack over the donuts, use oven mitts to flip the mold, and tap gently to release the donuts onto the parchment paper–lined rack to catch any frosting drippings.

While the donuts cool, prepare the glaze by whisking together the powdered sugar, strawberry powder, berry stevia, and plant-based milk until smooth. Drizzle the glaze over each donut, letting any excess drip off. Garnish with coconut flakes and/or fragrant dried rose petals or your favorite toppings before the glaze hardens.

Author's Note: Although this recipe includes white sugar, which may contribute to inflammation for some individuals, consider enjoying these donuts as a special treat on occasion, similar to how you might savor a slice of birthday cake. Moderation is key. This recipe also uses white flour, which may cause inflammation in some individuals. Pay attention to how your body responds and use your best judgment to determine what works best for you.

You can customize your donuts by replacing strawberry powder with blueberry, or topping them with crushed peanuts or vibrant sprinkles.

Understanding Sugar & Glycemic Index (GI)

The glycemic index (GI) measures how quickly a food raises blood sugar levels. Glucose, with a GI of 100, is the reference point. Here are the GI values of some common sugars that may lead to inflammation and other health issues:

- **Corn syrup (GI: 75):** A sweetener made from cornstarch, commonly used in processed foods and beverages.
- **Dextrose (GI: 100):** Also known as glucose, it is derived from starch and is used in baking and as a sweetener.
- **Fructose (GI: 19–25):** Although fructose has a lower GI, when consumed in excess, especially in isolated forms, it can lead to metabolic issues such as insulin resistance, fatty liver disease, and increased triglycerides. High-fructose corn syrup (HFCS) is a common isolated form.
- **Glucose (GI: 100):** The body's primary energy source, but excessive intake—especially from refined sources—can spike blood sugar and contribute to insulin resistance.
- **High-fructose corn syrup (GI: 55–55):** Processed corn syrup with a high fructose content, commonly used in soft drinks and processed foods.
- **Invert sugar (GI: 60):** A mixture of glucose and fructose, created by splitting sucrose into its component sugars.
- **Maltodextrin (GI: 85–105):** A processed starch used as a thickener or preservative and to improve mouthfeel in processed foods.
- **Maltose (GI: 105):** Also known as malt sugar, it is formed from two glucose molecules and is found in malted foods and beverages.
- **Rice syrup (GI: 98):** Derived from cooked rice, it is used as a sweetener in some natural and health food products.

- **Sucrose (GI: 65):** Commonly known as white table sugar, it is a disaccharide composed of glucose and fructose.
- **Maple syrup (GI: 54):** Contains some vitamins and minerals, like manganese and zinc, making it a slightly better option than refined sugars despite a similar GI.

Comparison of Agave Syrup and Maple Syrup

Agave Syrup

- **Fructose Content:** High (55–90 percent)
- **Glycemic Index (GI):** Low (19–30 percent)
- **Metabolic Impact:** High fructose content can lead to insulin resistance, fatty liver disease, and increased triglycerides.

Fructose is primarily metabolized by the liver, which can be overloaded with high fructose intake, leading to metabolic issues.

- **Nutritional Value:** Minimal vitamins and minerals
- **Processing:** Highly processed

Maple Syrup

- **Fructose Content:** Lower than agave syrup (contains sucrose, which is 50 percent fructose and 50 percent glucose)
- **Glycemic Index (GI):** Moderate (approximately 54)
- **Metabolic Impact:** More balanced glucose and fructose content, reducing the overload on the liver compared to high-fructose sweeteners. Lower likelihood of causing insulin resistance and fatty liver disease compared to high-fructose syrups.
  - **Nutritional Value:** Contains small amounts of vitamins and minerals like manganese, zinc, and antioxidants.
  - **Processing:** Less processed compared to many other sweeteners

Why Maple Syrup is Considered Better
- **Balanced Sugars:** Maple syrup contains a more balanced ratio of glucose and fructose, which reduces the strain on the liver compared to high-fructose sweeteners like agave syrup.
- **Lower Metabolic Risk:** The lower fructose content in maple syrup means it is less likely to contribute to insulin resistance, fatty liver disease, and increased triglycerides when consumed in moderation.
- **Nutritional Benefits:** Maple syrup contains small amounts of beneficial nutrients and antioxidants, such as manganese, zinc, and polyphenols, which are present in higher quantities than in agave syrup.
- **Processing:** Maple syrup is less processed than agave syrup, making it a more natural choice.

While agave syrup has a lower glycemic index, which means it causes a slower rise in blood sugar levels, its high fructose content can pose significant metabolic risks if consumed in excess. On the other hand, maple syrup, with its more balanced sugar content and additional nutrients, presents a lower risk for these metabolic issues and offers nutritional benefits, making it a generally better choice for overall health when used in moderation.

Clarification on Maple Syrup vs. Table Sugar
While maple syrup and table sugar (sucrose) have similar GIs, there are other factors to consider:
- **Nutritional Content:** Maple syrup contains small amounts of vitamins and minerals, such as manganese and zinc, which are not present in table sugar. These nutrients can provide slight health benefits.
- **Processing:** Maple syrup is less processed than refined table sugar, making it a more natural choice.
- **Flavor Profile:** The distinctive flavor of maple syrup allows you to use less of it to achieve the desired sweetness and taste.

Clarification on Maple Syrup vs. Agave Syrup

- **Glycemic Index (GI):** Agave syrup has a lower GI (approximately 19–30) compared to maple syrup (approximately 54), meaning it causes a slower rise in blood sugar levels. However, despite its lower GI, agave syrup is high in fructose, which may have negative metabolic effects. In contrast, maple syrup contains more beneficial nutrients and lower fructose levels, making it a healthier choice overall.
- **Nutritional Content:** Maple syrup provides more vitamins, minerals, and antioxidants, making it a more wholesome choice when consumed in moderation.
- **Fructose Content:** Agave syrup is high in fructose (55–90 percent), which, when consumed in excess, may contribute to insulin resistance, fatty liver disease, and elevated triglycerides. In contrast, maple syrup contains a more balanced ratio of glucose and fructose, making it a potentially better option when consumed in moderation.

Health Implications

When choosing sweeteners, it's important to consider not just glycemic impact but also nutrient content and processing. While maple syrup has a GI similar to table sugar, its higher nutrient profile and minimal processing make it a preferable option in moderation. In contrast, despite its lower GI, agave syrup's high fructose content may pose health risks, further supporting maple syrup as the better choice.

Practical Tips

- **Moderation Is Key:** Regardless of the type of sugar, consuming sweeteners in moderation is important to minimize health risks.
- **Whole Foods First:** Prioritize whole, unprocessed foods over sweeteners, even those with a lower GI or additional nutrients.
- **Read Labels:** Be aware of the types and amounts of sugars in processed foods to make informed choices.

By understanding the nuances of different sugars, including their GI and nutritional content, you can make more informed decisions that help manage inflammation and support overall health. Remember, moderation and a balanced diet are key to maintaining well-being. When choosing between maple syrup and other sweeteners like agave syrup or table sugar, consider the overall health benefits, nutrient content, and potential risks associated with each option.

Disclaimer:
Glycemic index (GI) values are based on research but may vary between individuals, sources, and food samples. Factors such as the distribution of sugars in natural foods and preparation methods (e.g., baked vs. raw potatoes) can influence GI levels. GI values are calculated for 100-gram servings, which may not align with typical portion sizes. Consuming high-GI foods with protein, fiber, or fat can lower their glycemic impact. While GI and glycemic load can assist in managing blood sugar levels and achieving specific health goals, consult your doctor before making significant dietary changes.

Contributors

Joshua Flint, John De La Mora, Michelle De La Mora, Pamela Wiley, Tony Mangiameli

A heartfelt thank-you to everyone who made our photo shoot a success. Joshua Flint, our amazing photographer, and his wife Ruqaiya AlBarwani Flint, for her invaluable assistance with staging and creative ideas. John De La Mora, my husband, for his unwavering support and kindness. Pamela Wiley, whose Thyme For Home Décor skills transformed our kitchen with her artistic touch. Tony and Crystal Mangiameli, for graciously offering their stunning kitchen overlooking the bluffs of Jasper Highlands. Your contributions truly brought this project to life.

John Del—Fried & Abuela's Baked Sopes

Indulge in Abuela's Sopes, a loving tribute to authentic Mexican flavors by John Del, inspired by his grandmother's cherished recipes. Each bite delivers an immersive taste of tradition, whisking you to the heart of Mexico. Savor the true essence of Mexican cuisine with a fiesta curated by John Del himself.

Scott Savage—24-Carrot Gold & Green Spaghetti

Recipe inspired by my son, Scott Savage, a natural chef. In the world of culinary artistry, Scott crafts unique blends with a passion for flavors. His imaginative touch brings each creation to life, making them both distinctive and memorable.

Arthur Savage—Tiki Love Potion & Barbecue Alternative to Blazing Buffalo Cauliflower with Blue Cheese Crumbles

Arthur's fondness for barbecue sauce at the tender age of three inspired this delicious variation. His early appreciation for flavors adds a personal touch to this recipe, showcasing his budding culinary preferences.

Curt Smith—Resourceful Dad Extraordinaire

A master problem solver and fellow info enthusiast, Curt has a knack for tackling any challenge. He's also the genius behind the photo editing in the spoon images.

Janelle Orlando—Orlando Tomato Soup

Jeannie Gagney—Pico de Gallo

Jeannie began her art career in Rock Island, Tennessee, where she resides. She draws inspiration from nature, capturing source photos during hiking and kayaking. Jeannie is passionate about her art and the joy that it brings her, and even more so, the joy it brings others.

    To find out more, visit Jeannie Gagney Art Studio on Facebook and Instagram.

Chuck Jones—coffee courtesy of Chuck Jones, CEO of The Lawman Rub Co., featured in Chaga Frappé & Spicy Cinnamon & Coffee Chili

The creative force behind The Lawman Rub Co., Chuck Jones, infuses his passion for coffee and barbecue seasonings into every product. Based in Knoxville, Tennessee, The Lawman Rub Co. is a family-owned business renowned for its exceptional quality and flavor. Chuck's dedication to excellence shines through in the Chaga Frappé and Spicy Cinnamon & Coffee Chili recipes.

Carrie Fritz—Avocado Margarita

A dedicated marathon runner with more than fifteen years of experience and a specialist in functional fitness, Carrie Fritz presents a refreshing twist on the classic margarita. With an emphasis on clean, health-conscious ingredients, this summer beverage is perfect for boosting any poolside gathering or summer party.

Catherine Sandoz—Ratatouille

Catherine Sandoz of Nurse Cat, LLC, is an Aesthetic Nurse Practitioner who has been injecting clients' faces for the past twenty years. She has A-list clients in Hollywood and Nashville, and has been instructing other medical professionals learning facial injecting for more than ten years.

Master Aesthetic Injecting Instructor
Concierge Medical Spa Service
Botox & Dermal Fillers
IV Hydration & Vitamin Infusions
Los Angeles, California
& TN, GA, SC, LA, KY, WV
(337) 207.8747
catsmobilebotox@gmail.com

Dori Orwig—Tennessee Killer Bread

As a Northern California native, Dori Orwig grew up enjoying authentic San Francisco sourdough bread. Now, as the owner of Tennessee Killer Breads, she highlights the health benefits of her sourdough,  made with only three ingredients: 100 percent organic and freshly milled unbleached flours, water, and sea salt. This naturally fermented bread has a deep, satisfying flavor and is easily digestible due to its reduced gluten content. Dori also loves creating versatile and party-pleasing bread sticks from the starter discard, adding any flavor to suit the mood.

Jen from Lean Bellas Kitchen—Fun Orange Treats

Jen is a culinary instructor with a practical, hands-on, and interactive teaching approach. She adapts her lessons to different skill levels and dietary needs, guiding both beginners and seasoned home cooks through the process of preparing healthy, satisfying meals.

Joshua Flint—Photographer, and Roqaiya AlBarwani Flint—Photography Assistant

jfphotos.myportfolio.com.

Roqaiya, Joshua's wife, plays a crucial role in the photo shoot, assisting with staging, ensuring every detail is perfect, and helping with creative ideas. Her keen eye for detail and supportive presence contribute significantly to the quality and success of the images.

Pamela Wiley—Designer and Inspiration Behind Thyme For Home Décor

Raised on a cattle farm in Ohio, Pam Wiley discovered her natural talent for design early on, despite it not being a family focus. With no formal training, she refined her skills over the years, guided by her faith.

Pam's life took a profound turn with the loss of her youngest son, JB, a beloved college student. In his honor, she opened Thyme For Home Décor on March 4—JB's birthday—a heartfelt tribute to his memory and the joy he brought to others.

Now living in Tennessee with her husband, Larry, Pam uses her creativity as a way to connect with others, offering comfort and encouragement to women who have faced similar losses. Her compassionate spirit and eye for design bring warmth and meaning to every space she touches.

Rachel Feldman—Chia Seed Pudding with Almond Butter
Sandra Ganis—Greek Salad

Inspired by her grandmother's wisdom and cherished Greek Salad, Sandra Ganis holds her heritage close to her heart. When Sandra was growing up in New York, her grandmother's insights into the health benefits of this traditional dish left a lasting impression. Now residing in Jasper Highlands, Tennessee, Sandra, at age fifty-eight, remains remarkably healthy, a testament to her grandmother's teachings. Her grandmother's strong belief in natural health remedies and avoidance of modern medicine, living until ninety-four without ever seeing a doctor, deeply influences Sandra's philosophy. Sandra proudly embraces her roots, prioritizing natural health remedies and demonstrating resilience, vitality, and the enduring bond between generations.

Sarah Bond—Eggplant Bacon & Vegan Pepperoni

Sarah Bond is the vegetarian food blogger behind the popular website Live Eat Learn. She uses her degrees in nutrition and food science to inspire healthy, approachable recipes that don't compromise on flavor. A traveler at heart based in Denver, her experiences around the globe give rise to unique and delicious flavor combinations.

J. Marchini Farms—Radicchio Rosa Salad

This recipe was created by J. Marchini Farms, a fourth-generation family farm in California's Central Valley specializing in radicchio and Italian-grown produce. For more information, visit jmarchinifarms.com.

Lisa and Emma Stewart—Cali Almond Flour Crackers & Pistachio Mint Hummus

Lisa and Emma Stewart created these delicious recipes, drawing inspiration from their J. Marchini Family Farm. Their time spent cooking together, particularly when Emma is home from Texas Christian University, underscores their strong mother-daughter bond and dedication to quality ingredients. While Emma is studying Communication and Spanish, Lisa and her husband, Adam, cultivate almonds and pistachios in Central California, bringing the best of their farm to the table.

Michael Nuccio—Coconut Date Energy Bites & Electrolyte Tropical Smoothie

Michael Nuccio, a UCLA student with a passion for health and wellness, focuses on helping people achieve optimal well-being. He views common issues like brain fog, bloating, and fatigue as signals that our bodies need more of the right nutrients. Michael believes that food provides essential raw materials for proper bodily function and that understanding this can lead to a healthier, more vibrant life. Through his knowledge of nutrition and exercise, he aims to enhance

Contributors

people's quality of life. For more health tips and inspiration, follow him on Instagram @nuccio.health.

The Creature Preachers—The Creature Preachers' Black Cauldron Chili

The Creature Preachers are a horror surf rock band from Warner Robins, GA, blending classic surf rock with high energy vibes. The band recently debuted their album "Necro A-Go-Go" across all major streaming platforms, quickly building a fanbase with their distinctive sound. Their live shows, including shows and festivals across Georgia and the Southeast, deliver a thrilling experience for fans of both surf and horror music. The lineup includes: Gage the Mage on keys and vocals, Greg Regular on guitar and vocals, Overkill Will on bass, and Drum Phil on drums.

Tony Mangiameli—Mangiameli Family Sauce

Tony Mangiameli's cherished spaghetti sauce traces its roots back to Tony's family in Sicily, dating back to the early 1800s. The recipe has been passed down through generations: Tony's great-grandfather, Salvatore Mangiameli, to his grandfather Giovanni, then to his father Lenny and so on.

Today, Tony proudly continues the legacy, infusing the recipe with the same passion that has endured for centuries. To set the mood, he suggests playing old Italian music, perhaps tunes by Frank Sinatra or Dean Martin, or the melodic sounds of Louis Prima, creating a smile and a sense of nostalgia.

Essential tools include a dish towel, known as a "mapine" in Italian culture, draped over the left shoulder if you're right-handed, for easy access to wipe hands while working with garlic and sauce. Additionally, a wooden spoon is indispensable for stirring and blending the ingredients, despite any childhood memories it may evoke.

For more information, contact Tony Mangiameli at Mangiameli Farmers Insurance: mangiameli@sbcglobal.net.

Resources

Salt and Electrolytes
An Analysis of the Mineral Composition of Pink Salt
PMC PubMed Central
https://www.ncbi.nlm.nih.gov/pmc/articles/PMC7603209/

Electrolytes
Cleveland Clinic
https://my.clevelandclinic.org/health/diagnostics/21790-electrolytes

Sole Himalayan Salt Drinking Therapy
Indego Health Clinic
https://www.indigohealthclinic.com/sole-himalayan-salt/

The Downside of a Low Salt Diet
Mark Hyman M.D.
https://drhyman.com/blogs/content/downside-low-salt-diet

The Salt Fix: Why the Experts Got It All Wrong . . .
Dr. James DiNicolantonio
https://www.drjamesdinic.com/

Habit Formation
Phillippa Lally et al.
https://www.ncbi.nlm.nih.gov/pmc/articles/PMC3505409/

Plant-Based Diets
How Not to Die by Dr. Michael Greger
The China Study by Dr. T. Colin Campbell and Thomas M. Campbell II

Sugar Information
Harvard T.H. Chan School of Public Health
https://nutritionsource.hsph.harvard.edu/healthy-drinks/sugary-drinks/

American Heart Association (AHA)
AHA offers guidelines on sugar intake and its relationship with heart health and inflammation. AHA: Sugar 101
https://www.heart.org/en/healthy-living/healthy-eating/eat-smart/sugar

Diabetes Management
American Diabetes Association (ADA)
Healthy Food Choices Made Easy
Guidelines on managing diabetes and hypoglycemia, including monitoring high-glycemic foods and understanding their impact on blood sugar levels.
https://www.diabetes.org/nutrition

Carbohydrates and Blood Sugar
Harvard T.H. Chan School of Public Health
Glycemic index and its role in managing blood sugar levels, especially for diabetes and hypoglycemia.
https://nutritionsource.hsph.harvard.edu/carbohydrates/carbohydrates-and-blood-sugar/

Inflammatory Diseases
Arthritis Foundation: Are Nightshades Bad for Arthritis?
The impact of nightshades and gluten on inflammatory diseases such as autoimmune diseases, lupus, and rheumatoid arthritis.
https://www.arthritis.org/health-wellness/healthy-living/nutrition/anti-inflammatory/how-nightshades-affect-arthritis

Harvard Health Publishing
Going Gluten-Free Just Because
The effects of gluten on autoimmune diseases and inflammation.
https://www.health.harvard.edu/staying-healthy/ditch-the-gluten-improve-your-health

Kidney Stone Prevention
National Kidney Foundation
Guidelines on managing kidney stones by limiting high-oxalate foods.
https://www.kidney.org/atoz/content/kidneystones

SIBO (Small Intestinal Bacteria Overgrowth)
Mayo Clinic
Information on small intestinal bacterial overgrowth (SIBO) and its dietary management.
https://www.mayoclinic.org/diseases-conditions/small-intestinal-bacterial-overgrowth/symptoms-causes/syc-20370168

IBS (Irritable Bowel Syndrome)
International Foundation for Gastrointestinal Disorders (IFFGD)
Comprehensive information on irritable bowel syndrome (IBS) and its dietary considerations.
https://iffgd.org/gi-disorders/lower-gi-disorders/irritable-bowel-syndrome/

Candida
Mayo Clinic—Candidiasis
Overview and management of candidiasis, including dietary considerations.
https://www.mayoclinic.org/healthy-lifestyle/consumer-health/expert-answers/candida-cleanse/faq-20058174

Acknowledgments

Resources and knowledge provided in this book are grounded in extensive coursework and specialized training from renowned programs, including:

Qualifications: Certified Brain Health Professional from Amen Clinics and Certified Integrative Nutrition Health Coach, with specialized training in gut health.

Training and Education: Professional certification from Amen University, under the mentorship of Dr. Daniel G. Amen, and The Institute for Integrative Nutrition in New York City, led by Joshua Rosenthal, Founder and Director.

These credentials ensure that the recommendations and practices in this book are rooted in comprehensive, evidence-based knowledge for optimal health and wellness.

Metric Conversions

If you're accustomed to using metric measurements, use these handy charts to convert the imperial measurements used in this book.

Weight (Dry Ingredients)

1 oz		30 g
4 oz	¼ lb	120 g
8 oz	½ lb	240 g
12 oz	¾ lb	360 g
16 oz	1 lb	480 g
32 oz	2 lb	960 g

Volume (Liquid Ingredients)

½ tsp.		2 ml
1 tsp.		5 ml
1 Tbsp.	½ fl oz	15 ml
2 Tbsp.	1 fl oz	30 ml
¼ cup	2 fl oz	60 ml
⅓ cup	3 fl oz	80 ml
½ cup	4 fl oz	120 ml
⅔ cup	5 fl oz	160 ml
¾ cup	6 fl oz	180 ml
1 cup	8 fl oz	240 ml
1 pt	16 fl oz	480 ml
1 qt	32 fl oz	960 ml

Oven Temperatures

Fahrenheit	Celsius	Gas Mark
225°	110°	¼
250°	120°	½
275°	140°	1
300°	150°	2
325°	160°	3
350°	180°	4
375°	190°	5
400°	200°	6
425°	220°	7
450°	230°	8

Length

¼ in	6 mm
½ in	13 mm
¾ in	19 mm
1 in	25 mm
6 in	15 cm
12 in	30 cm

Index

A

Abuela's Fried Sopes, 157–158
agave, 260, 262
    Fit Fritz Avocado Margarita, 247
aioli
    Spicy Garlic Aioli, 234
almond butter
    Chia Seed Pudding with Almond Butter, 76
    Messy Loaded Almond Yogurt & Banana Nut Crunch, 73
    Raspberry & Cardamom Smoothie, 60
    Salted Caramel Fondue, 219
almond flour
    Cali Almond Flour Crackers, 101–102
    Fuel Bombs, 105
almond milk
    vanilla
        Raspberry & Cardamom Smoothie, 60
almonds
    Messy Loaded Almond Yogurt & Banana Nut Crunch, 73
    Roasted Rosemary Naked Almonds, 96
Aloha Kakahiaka Overnight Oats, 79
Anaheim pepper
    Chipotle Sauce, 235
    Spicy Chorizo Tacos, 80
ancho pepper
    Spicy Aztec Soup, 117–119
appetite, 34
apple
    Chia Seed Pudding with Almond Butter, 76
    No-Crab Crab Cakes, 94
apple juice
    Pear Jam, 153
    Spicy Mango Salad, 133
artichoke hearts
    Lemon Zoodles, Capers & Empress Tomatoes, 192
arugula
    Carb-Free Pizza Bowl, 187
    Creamy Caprese Seduction, 127–128
    Lemon Zoodles, Capers & Empress Tomatoes, 192
    Spicy Chorizo Tacos, 80
Arugula Linguine with Lemon Zest & Capers, 193
avocado
    Chimichurri Chickpea & Avocado Sandwich, 149
    Fit Fritz Avocado Margarita, 247
    Green Spaghetti, 175–176
    Spicy Mango Salad, 133

B

bacon
    Eggplant Bacon, 241
banana
    Aloha Kakahiaka Overnight Oats, 79
    Chia Seed Pudding with Almond Butter, 76
    Chocolate Bananasicles, 223
    Cocoa Jungle Monkey Mousse, 210
    Electrolyte Tropical Smoothie, 63
Barbecue Italian Beyond® Loaf, 163
barbecue sauce
    Barbecue Italian Beyond® Loaf, 163
    Pulled Lion's Mane Slaw Burger, 164–167
basil
    Cashew Basil Blitz, 173–174
    Creamy Caprese Seduction, 127–128
    Green Spaghetti, 175–176
    Lemon Zoodles, Capers & Empress Tomatoes, 192
    Mangiameli's Family Spaghetti Sauce, 168–169
    Orlando Tomato Soup, 111–112
bay leaves
    Spicy Cinnamon & Coffee Chili, 120–122
beans, 27
    black
        Bold Border Sauce, 182
        Creature Preachers' Black Cauldron Chili, 114
        Golden Spice Puff Pockets, 159–160
    kidney
        Creature Preachers' Black Cauldron Chili, 114
        Spicy Cinnamon & Coffee Chili, 120–122
    Spicy Aztec Soup, 117–119
bean sprouts
    PhoMazing Soup, 115–116
beef
    Beyond
        Barbecue Italian Beyond® Loaf, 163
        Rustic Cornbread Skillet, 185–186
bell pepper
    Barbecue Italian Beyond® Loaf, 163
    Boston Baked Lentils, 190–191
    Carb-Free Pizza Bowl, 187
    Creature Preachers' Black Cauldron Chili, 114
    Crispy Garden Rolls with Hoisin Glazed Dipping Sauce, 134–136
    Parmesan Polenta & Mushrooms, 181
    Peanut & Cashew Asian Stir-Fry, 196–198
    PhoMazing Soup, 115–116
    Ratatouille, 177
    Rustic Cornbread Skillet, 185–186
    Spicy Chorizo Tacos, 80
    Spicy Cinnamon & Coffee Chili, 120–122
Berry Chia Dream, 74
beverages
    Chaga Frappé, 66
    Chaga & Hawthorn Berry Tea, 64
    Chamomile & Pink Lemonade Kombucha Fizz, 51
    Electrolyte Fruit Punch, 49
    Electrolyte Tropical Smoothie, 63
    Fire & Fluxx, 59
    Fit Fritz Avocado Margarita, 247
    Lemon Drop Healing Tonic, 65
    Raspberry & Cardamom Smoothie, 60
    Rose Petal Elixir, 47
    Sole, 48
    Sparkling Blood Orange Root Beer, 56
    Sparkling Chocolate Blueberries & Mint Elixir, 55
    Tiki Love Potion, 52
Blazing Buffalo Cauliflower with Blue Cheese Crumbles, 147–148
blender, 11
    immersion, 12
Blistering Shishitos with Feta & Fiesta Smoked Crème, 92
blueberries
    frozen
        Cherry Sorbet, 213
    Sparkling Chocolate Blueberries & Mint Elixir, 55
blueberry juice
    Sparkling Chocolate Blueberries & Mint Elixir, 55
bok choy
    PhoMazing Soup, 115–116
Bold Border Sauce, 182
Boston Baked Lentils, 190–191
bread
    Chimichurri Chickpea & Avocado Sandwich, 149
    Dutch Oven Cheesy Jalapeño Artisan Bread, 254
    Jalapeño Pizza Crunch Melt, 125–126

Rustic Cornbread Skillet, 185–186
Savory Tofu Scramble on Sun-Dried Slathered Toast, 84–86
sourdough, 30, 152
breakfast
   Aloha Kakahiaka Overnight Oats, 79
   Berry Chia Dream, 74
   Cheesy Jalapeño Pop'n Breakfast Cups, 71
   Chia Seed Pudding with Almond Butter, 76
   Easy Skillet Breakfast Potatoes, 72
   Maple Almond Chocolate Chip Overnight Oats, 76
   Messy Loaded Almond Yogurt & Banana Nut Crunch, 73
   Savory Tofu Scramble on Sun-Dried Slathered Toast, 84–86
   Spicy Chorizo Tacos, 80
   Spicy Red Lentil Tortillas, 83
   Sun-Kissed Capers & Squash, 87
broccoli
   Peanut & Cashew Asian Stir-Fry, 196–198
   Spicy Mango Salad, 133
   White Cheddar & Broccoli, 145
buffalo sauce, 19
Buffalo sauce
   Blazing Buffalo Cauliflower with Blue Cheese Crumbles, 147–148
buns
   Pulled Lion's Mane Slaw Burger, 164–167
burger
   Pulled Lion's Mane Slaw Burger, 164–167
butter, 19

C

cabbage
   Pulled Lion's Mane Slaw Burger, 164–167
cacao butter
   Luxurious Chocolate Masterpieces, 216–217
   Rocky Road Fudge, 209
cacao powder
   Chaga Frappé, 66
   Cocoa Jungle Monkey Mousse, 210
   Luxurious Chocolate Masterpieces, 216–217
   Rocky Road Fudge, 209
   Truffle Joy Bombs, 214
   Ultimate Tsunami Cacao, 226
Cali Almond Flour Crackers, 101–102
candida, 26
capers
   Arugula Linguine with Lemon Zest & Capers, 193
   Pasta alla Bella Capri, 195
   Sun-Kissed Capers & Squash, 87

Carb-Free Pizza Bowl, 187
cardamom
   Raspberry & Cardamom Smoothie, 60
cardamom pods
   Rose Petal Elixir, 47
carrots
   Creature Preachers' Black Cauldron Chili, 114
   Crispy Garden Rolls with Hoisin Glazed Dipping Sauce, 134–136
   Golden Spice Puff Pockets, 159–160
   Mangiameli's Family Spaghetti Sauce, 168–169
   Orlando Tomato Soup, 111–112
   Pulled Lion's Mane Slaw Burger, 164–167
   Radicchio Rosa Salad, 141
   24-Carrot Gold, 91
   Zen Garden Salad with Sesame-Lime Dressing, 130–131
Cashew Basil Blitz, 173–174
cashew butter
   Messy Loaded Almond Yogurt & Banana Nut Crunch, 73
   Salted Caramel Fondue, 219
Cashew Crèma Mexicana, 232
   Green Spaghetti, 175–176
   Spicy Chorizo Tacos, 80
Cashew Crème Fraîche, 178
cashew milk
   Garlic Mashed Potatoes & Sweet Corn, 144
cashews
   Cashew Basil Blitz, 173–174
   Chilled Tofu Mac, 137–139
   Chipotle Sauce, 235
   Creamy Caprese Seduction, 127–128
   Nutty Parmesan, 233
   Spicy Garlic Aioli, 234
cauliflower
   Blazing Buffalo Cauliflower with Blue Cheese Crumbles, 147–148
cayenne
   Cashew Basil Blitz, 173–174
   Creature Preachers' Black Cauldron Chili, 114
   Fire & Flux, 59
   Golden Spice Puff Pockets, 159–160
   Reishi Mushroom Turmeric Latte, 226
   Savory Tofu Scramble on Sun-Dried Slathered Toast, 84–86
   Spicy Moroccan Loaded Sweet Potato, 199
celery
   Barbecue Italian Beyond® Loaf, 163
   Chilled Tofu Mac, 137–139
   No-Crab Crab Cakes, 94
   Peanut & Cashew Asian Stir-Fry, 196–198

PhoMazing Soup, 115–116
Spicy Aztec Soup, 117–119
Spicy Cinnamon & Coffee Chili, 120–122
Zen Garden Salad with Sesame-Lime Dressing, 130–131
chaga
   Chaga & Hawthorn Berry Tea, 64
Chaga Frappé, 66
Chaga & Hawthorn Berry Tea, 64
Chamomile & Pink Lemonade Kombucha Fizz, 51
cheese, 19–21
   blue
      Blazing Buffalo Cauliflower with Blue Cheese Crumbles, 147–148
      Dutch Oven Cheesy Jalapeño Artisan Bread, 254
   feta
      Ganis's Greek Salad, 142
      Pickled Tofu Feta, 244
   gouda
      Fire-Kissed Gouda Bites, 100
   Mexican
      Cheesy Jalapeño Pop'n Breakfast Cups, 71
   mozzarella, 22
      Jalapeño Pizza Crunch Melt, 125–126
   Parmesan
      Parmesan Polenta & Mushrooms, 181
cheese spread, 20
Cheesy Jalapeño Pop'n Breakfast Cups, 71
cherries
   dried, 22
      Fuel Bombs, 105
      Messy Loaded Almond Yogurt & Banana Nut Crunch, 73
   frozen
      Cherry Sorbet, 213
   maraschino
      Tiki Love Potion, 52
cherry juice
   Tiki Love Potion, 52
Cherry Sorbet, 213
Chia Seed Pudding with Almond Butter, 76
chia seeds
   Berry Chia Dream, 74
   Maple Almond Chocolate Chip Overnight Oats, 76
   Messy Loaded Almond Yogurt & Banana Nut Crunch, 73
   Pear Jam, 153
chickpeas
   Chimichurri Chickpea & Avocado Sandwich, 149

No-Crab Crab Cakes, 94
Pistachio Mint Hummus, 106
chili
    Creature Preachers' Black Cauldron Chili, 114
    Spicy Cinnamon & Coffee Chili, 120-122
chili pepper
    Chimichurri Chickpea & Avocado Sandwich, 149
    Ratatouille, 177
chili powder
    Creature Preachers' Black Cauldron Chili, 114
    Spicy Aztec Soup, 117-119
    Spicy Cinnamon & Coffee Chili, 120-122
    24-Carrot Gold, 91
Chilled Tofu Mac, 137-139
Chimichurri Chickpea & Avocado Sandwich, 149
Chinese five-spice powder
    Crispy Garden Rolls with Hoisin Glazed Dipping Sauce, 134-136
    Peanut Sauce, 199
Chipotle Sauce, 235
    Spicy Chorizo Tacos, 80
chipotle seasoning
    Chipotle Sauce, 235
Chocolate Bananasicles, 223
chocolate chips
    dark
        Maple Almond Chocolate Chip Overnight Oats, 76
        Popcorn Paradise, 95
        Edible Maple Almond Chocolate Chip Oat Cookie Dough, 205
        Ultimate Tsunami Cacao, 226
chorizo
    Spicy Chorizo Tacos, 80
cilantro
    Crispy Garden Rolls with Hoisin Glazed Dipping Sauce, 134-136
    Golden Spice Puff Pockets, 159-160
    Pico de Gallo, 237
    Zen Garden Salad with Sesame-Lime Dressing, 130-131
cinnamon
    Chaga Frappé, 66
    Chia Seed Pudding with Almond Butter, 76
    Messy Loaded Almond Yogurt & Banana Nut Crunch, 73
    Raspberry & Cardamom Smoothie, 60
    Reishi Mushroom Turmeric Latte, 226
    Spicy Cinnamon & Coffee Chili, 120-122
    Ultimate Tsunami Cacao, 226
Cocoa Jungle Monkey Mousse, 210

cocoa powder
    Fuel Bombs, 105
    Rocky Road Fudge, 209
coconut
    flakes
        Aloha Kakahiaka Overnight Oats, 79
    shredded
        Coconut Date Energy Bites, 99
coconut aminos
    Maple-Smoked Plant Ribbons, 238
coconut cream
    Cocoa Jungle Monkey Mousse, 210
    Creamy Chanterelle Soup, 109-110
Coconut Date Energy Bites, 99
coconut milk
    Aloha Kakahiaka Overnight Oats, 79
    Chaga Frappé, 66
    Cherry Sorbet, 213
    Golden Milk, 225
    Reishi Mushroom Turmeric Latte, 226
coconut water
    Electrolyte Tropical Smoothie, 63
coffee
    Chaga Frappé, 66
    Spicy Cinnamon & Coffee Chili, 120-122
    Ultimate Tsunami Cacao, 226
cookies
    Edible Maple Almond Chocolate Chip Oat Cookie Dough, 205
    Maple Almond Chocolate Chip Oat Cookie Dough Pops, 206
coriander
    Spicy Cinnamon & Coffee Chili, 120-122
corn
    Bold Border Sauce, 182
    Creature Preachers' Black Cauldron Chili, 114
    Garlic Mashed Potatoes & Sweet Corn, 144
    masa
        Abuela's Fried Sopes, 157-158
        Rustic Cornbread Skillet, 185-186
        Spicy Cinnamon & Coffee Chili, 120-122
cornbread
    Rustic Cornbread Skillet, 185-186
corn syrup, 259
crab cakes
    No-Crab Crab Cakes, 94
crackers
    Cali Almond Flour Crackers, 101-102
    Triscuit tomato & olive oil Fire-Kissed Gouda Bites, 100
cranberries, dried
    Fuel Bombs, 105
    Popcorn Paradise, 95

cravings, 43-44
Creamy Caprese Seduction, 127-128
Creamy Chanterelle Soup, 109-110
Creature Preachers' Black Cauldron Chili, 114
Crispy Garden Rolls with Hoisin Glazed Dipping Sauce, 134-136
Crispy Sourdough Bread Sticks, 150
cucumber
    English
        Crispy Garden Rolls with Hoisin Glazed Dipping Sauce, 134-136
        Ganis's Greek Salad, 142
        Spicy Mango Salad, 133
cumin
    Creature Preachers' Black Cauldron Chili, 114
    Golden Spice Puff Pockets, 159-160
    Spicy Aztec Soup, 117-119
    Spicy Cinnamon & Coffee Chili, 120-122
    Spicy Moroccan Loaded Sweet Potato, 199

D
dates
    Coconut Date Energy Bites, 99
dextrose, 259
diabetes, 26-27
dill
    Chilled Tofu Mac, 137-139
    No-Crab Crab Cakes, 94
    Prosecco Pickled Jalapeños, 242
donuts
    Strawberry Fields Forever Donuts, 256-258
Dutch oven, 11, 12
Dutch Oven Cheesy Jalapeño Artisan Bread, 254

E
Easy Flour Tortillas, 253
Easy Skillet Breakfast Potatoes, 72
edamame
    Zen Garden Salad with Sesame-Lime Dressing, 130-131
Edible Maple Almond Chocolate Chip Oat Cookie Dough, 205
eggplant
    Chinese
        Ratatouille, 177
    Roasted Eggplant Tzatziki, 188
Eggplant Bacon, 241
eggs, 22
    Cheesy Jalapeño Pop'n Breakfast Cups, 71
Electrolyte Fruit Punch, 49
Electrolyte Tropical Smoothie, 63
erythritol, 28

F

Fire & Flux, 59
Fire-Kissed Gouda Bites, 100
Fit Fritz Avocado Margarita, 247
flaxseed meal
    Cali Almond Flour Crackers, 101–102
flaxseeds
    Fuel Bombs, 105
fondue
    Salted Caramel Fondue, 219
food processor, 11
fructose, 259
fudge
    Rocky Road Fudge, 209
Fuel Bombs, 105
Fun Orange Treats, 224

G

Ganis's Greek Salad, 142
garam masala
    Golden Spice Puff Pockets, 159–160
garlic
    Blistering Shishitos with Feta & Fiesta Smoked Crème, 92
    Cashew Basil Blitz, 173–174
    Cashew Crème Fraîche, 178
    Chilled Tofu Mac, 137–139
    Chimichurri Chickpea & Avocado Sandwich, 149
    Chipotle Sauce, 235
    Creamy Caprese Seduction, 127–128
    Creamy Chanterelle Soup, 109–110
    Creature Preachers' Black Cauldron Chili, 114
    Crispy Garden Rolls with Hoisin Glazed Dipping Sauce, 134–136
    Easy Skillet Breakfast Potatoes, 72
    Ganis's Greek Salad, 142
    Garlic Mashed Potatoes & Sweet Corn, 144
    Golden Spice Puff Pockets, 159–160
    Mangiameli's Family Spaghetti Sauce, 168–169
    Orlando Tomato Soup, 111–112
    Pasta alla Bella Capri, 195
    Peanut & Cashew Asian Stir-Fry, 196–198
    Peanut Sauce, 199
    Pico de Gallo, 237
    Pistachio Mint Hummus, 106
    Prosecco Pickled Jalapeños, 242
    Ratatouille, 177
    Rustic Cornbread Skillet, 185–186
    Savory Tofu Scramble on Sun-Dried Slathered Toast, 84–86
    Spicy Chorizo Tacos, 80
    Spicy Cinnamon & Coffee Chili, 120–122
    Spicy Garlic Aioli, 234
    Spicy Moroccan Loaded Sweet Potato, 199
    Zen Garden Salad with Sesame-Lime Dressing, 130–131
Garlic Mashed Potatoes & Sweet Corn, 144
garlic powder
    Barbecue Italian Beyond® Loaf, 163
    Blazing Buffalo Cauliflower with Blue Cheese Crumbles, 147–148
    Cali Almond Flour Crackers, 101–102
    Creature Preachers' Black Cauldron Chili, 114
    Savory Tofu Scramble on Sun-Dried Slathered Toast, 84–86
    Spicy Aztec Soup, 117–119
    Spicy Cinnamon & Coffee Chili, 120–122
    24-Carrot Gold, 91
    White Cheddar & Broccoli, 145
ginger
    Crispy Garden Rolls with Hoisin Glazed Dipping Sauce, 134–136
    Golden Spice Puff Pockets, 159–160
    Lemon Drop Healing Tonic, 65
    Peanut & Cashew Asian Stir-Fry, 196–198
    Peanut Sauce, 199
    PhoMazing Soup, 115–116
    Reishi Mushroom Turmeric Latte, 226
    Zen Garden Salad with Sesame-Lime Dressing, 130–131
glucose, 259
gluten, 27, 30
    Vegan Pepperoni, 250
glycemic index (GI), 259–263
Golden Milk, 225
Golden Spice Puff Pockets, 159–160
grains, 27, 30
Greek seasoning
    Parmesan Polenta & Mushrooms, 181
green chili peppers
    Creature Preachers' Black Cauldron Chili, 114
    Spicy Red Lentil Tortillas, 83
Green Spaghetti, 175–176
guajillo pepper
    Spicy Aztec Soup, 117–119

H

hawthorn berries
    Chaga & Hawthorn Berry Tea, 64
hummus
    Pistachio Mint Hummus, 106
hunger, 34
hypoglycemia, 26–27

I

IBS, 27–28
immunity, 29
inflammation, 15, 23, 24, 26–29, 31–32, 40–41
inflammatory diseases, 27
intuitiveness, 34
Italian seasoning
    Barbecue Italian Beyond® Loaf, 163
    Cashew Crème Fraîche, 178
    Chilled Tofu Mac, 137–139
    Mangiameli's Family Spaghetti Sauce, 168–169

J

jalapeño
    Dutch Oven Cheesy Jalapeño Artisan Bread, 254
    Jalapeño Pizza Crunch Melt, 125–126
    Pico de Gallo, 237
    Prosecco Pickled Jalapeños, 242
    Ratatouille, 177
    Rustic Cornbread Skillet, 185–186
    Zen Garden Salad with Sesame-Lime Dressing, 130–131
Jalapeño Pizza Crunch Melt, 125–126
jalapeños
    Cheesy Jalapeño Pop'n Breakfast Cups, 71
jam
    Pear Jam, 153

K

kale
    Cashew Basil Blitz, 173–174
kidney stones, 27
kimchi
    No-Crab Crab Cakes, 94
    Spicy Mango Salad, 133
knife
    bread, 12
    paring, 11
kombu
    PhoMazing Soup, 115–116
kombucha
    Chamomile & Pink Lemonade Kombucha Fizz, 51

L

labels, 15, 32
lemon
    Cashew Basil Blitz, 173–174
    Lemon Drop Healing Tonic, 65
    Rose Petal Elixir, 47
Lemon Drop Healing Tonic, 65
lemon juice
    Arugula Linguine with Lemon Zest & Capers, 193
    Cashew Crème Fraîche, 178
    Chilled Tofu Mac, 137–139
    Fire & Flux, 59
    Lemon Zoodles, Capers & Empress Tomatoes, 192
    Pear Jam, 153

Pistachio Mint Hummus, 106
Spicy Garlic Aioli, 234
Spicy Moroccan Loaded Sweet
  Potato, 199
Strawberry Fields Forever Donuts,
  256–258
lemon zest
  Blistering Shishitos with Feta & Fiesta
    Smoked Crème, 92
Lemon Zoodles, Capers & Empress
  Tomatoes, 192
lentils
  Boston Baked Lentils, 190–191
  red
    Spicy Red Lentil Tortillas, 83
lettuce
  Crispy Garden Rolls with Hoisin
    Glazed Dipping Sauce, 134–136
  Zen Garden Salad with Sesame-Lime
    Dressing, 130–131
lime
  Crispy Garden Rolls with Hoisin
    Glazed Dipping Sauce, 134–136
  Fit Fritz Avocado Margarita, 247
  No-Crab Crab Cakes, 94
  Sparkling Chocolate Blueberries &
    Mint Elixir, 55
lime juice
  Abuela's Fried Sopes, 157–158
  Bold Border Sauce, 182
  Cashew Crèma Mexicana, 232
  Chipotle Sauce, 235
  Electrolyte Tropical Smoothie, 63
  Fit Fritz Avocado Margarita, 247
  Zen Garden Salad with Sesame-Lime
    Dressing, 130–131
liquid smoke
  Maple-Smoked Plant Ribbons, 238
  Vegan Pepperoni, 250
Luxurious Chocolate Masterpieces,
  216–217
  Chocolate Bananasicles, 223

M

maltodextrin, 259
maltose, 259
Mangiameli's Family Spaghetti Sauce,
  168–169
mango
  Aloha Kakahiaka Overnight Oats, 79
  Electrolyte Tropical Smoothie, 63
Maple Almond Chocolate Chip Oat
  Cookie Dough Pops, 206
Maple Almond Chocolate Chip
  Overnight Oats, 76
Maple-Smoked Plant Ribbons, 238
  Cheesy Jalapeño Pop'n Breakfast
    Cups, 71
maple syrup, 31, 260–262
  Aloha Kakahiaka Overnight Oats, 79

Boston Baked Lentils, 190–191
Cali Almond Flour Crackers, 101–102
Chaga Frappé, 66
Cherry Sorbet, 213
Chilled Tofu Mac, 137–139
Cocoa Jungle Monkey Mousse, 210
Crispy Garden Rolls with Hoisin
  Glazed Dipping Sauce, 134–136
Dutch Oven Cheesy Jalapeño Artisan
  Bread, 254
Edible Maple Almond Chocolate
  Chip Oat Cookie Dough, 205
Eggplant Bacon, 241
Fuel Bombs, 105
Lemon Drop Healing Tonic, 65
Luxurious Chocolate Masterpieces,
  216–217
Maple Almond Chocolate Chip
  Overnight Oats, 76
Maple-Smoked Plant Ribbons, 238
Peanut Sauce, 199
Prosecco Pickled Jalapeños, 242
Pulled Lion's Mane Slaw Burger,
  164–167
Rocky Road Fudge, 209
Rose Petal Elixir, 47
Rustic Cornbread Skillet, 185–186
Spicy Cinnamon & Coffee Chili,
  120–122
Spicy Moroccan Loaded Sweet
  Potato, 199
Strawberry Fields Forever Donuts,
  256–258
Truffle Joy Bombs, 214
Ultimate Tsunami Cacao, 226
Zen Garden Salad with Sesame-Lime
  Dressing, 130–131
margarine, 14
margarita
  Fit Fritz Avocado Margarita, 247
masa
  Abuela's Fried Sopes, 157–158
mayonnaise
  No-Crab Crab Cakes, 94
  Pulled Lion's Mane Slaw Burger,
    164–167
meat
  ground, 22
  pepperoni, 23
Messy Loaded Almond Yogurt & Banana
  Nut Crunch, 73
Mexican seasoning
  Bold Border Sauce, 182
  Cheesy Jalapeño Pop'n Breakfast
    Cups, 71
  Rustic Cornbread Skillet, 185–186
mint
  Ganis's Greek Salad, 142
  Pistachio Mint Hummus, 106

miso
  red
    Pasta alla Bella Capri, 195
  white
    PhoMazing Soup, 115–116
molasses
  Boston Baked Lentils, 190–191
molds, silicone, 12
mousse
  Cocoa Jungle Monkey Mousse, 210
mushrooms
  baby bella
    Creamy Chanterelle Soup, 109–110
  chanterelle
    Creamy Chanterelle Soup, 109–110
  cremini
    Spicy Moroccan Loaded Sweet
      Potato, 199
  lion's mane
    Pulled Lion's Mane Slaw Burger,
      164–167
  Parmesan Polenta & Mushrooms, 181
  PhoMazing Soup, 115–116
  reishi
    Reishi Mushroom Turmeric Latte,
      226
mustard
  Dijon
    Chilled Tofu Mac, 137–139
    Pulled Lion's Mane Slaw Burger,
      164–167
  No-Crab Crab Cakes, 94
mustard powder
  Spicy Garlic Aioli, 234
mustard seeds
  Barbecue Italian Beyond® Loaf, 163

N

Neapolitan-Style Pizza, 248–249
No-Crab Crab Cakes, 94
nori
  No-Crab Crab Cakes, 94
nutritional yeast, 21, 27
  Cashew Basil Blitz, 173–174
  Cashew Crèma Mexicana, 232
  Cashew Crème Fraîche, 178
  Chilled Tofu Mac, 137–139
  Creamy Caprese Seduction, 127–128
  Garlic Mashed Potatoes & Sweet
    Corn, 144
  Maple-Smoked Plant Ribbons, 238
  Nutty Parmesan, 233
nuts
  Fuel Bombs, 105
Nutty Parmesan, 233
  Lemon Zoodles, Capers & Empress
    Tomatoes, 192
  Pasta alla Bella Capri, 195
  White Cheddar & Broccoli, 145

O

oat milk
- Maple Almond Chocolate Chip Overnight Oats, 76
- Parmesan Polenta & Mushrooms, 181
- Strawberry Fields Forever Donuts, 256–258
- Ultimate Tsunami Cacao, 226

oats
- Aloha Kakahiaka Overnight Oats, 79
- Fuel Bombs, 105
- Maple Almond Chocolate Chip Overnight Oats, 76

oils, 13–14
- avocado, 14
- canola, 14
- coconut, 14
- margarine, 14
- olive, 14
- peanut, 14
- vegetable, 14

olives
- Castelvetrano
  - Pickled Tofu Feta, 244
- Greek
  - Lemon Zoodles, Capers & Empress Tomatoes, 192
- kalamata
  - Ganis's Greek Salad, 142
  - Lemon Zoodles, Capers & Empress Tomatoes, 192
  - Pasta alla Bella Capri, 195

onion
- Barbecue Italian Beyond® Loaf, 163
- Cashew Crème Fraîche, 178
- Chimichurri Chickpea & Avocado Sandwich, 149
- Creamy Chanterelle Soup, 109–110
- Creature Preachers' Black Cauldron Chili, 114
- crispy
  - Zen Garden Salad with Sesame-Lime Dressing, 130–131
- Crispy Garden Rolls with Hoisin Glazed Dipping Sauce, 134–136
- Easy Skillet Breakfast Potatoes, 72
- Ganis's Greek Salad, 142
- Golden Spice Puff Pockets, 159–160
- green
  - Crispy Garden Rolls with Hoisin Glazed Dipping Sauce, 134–136
  - Garlic Mashed Potatoes & Sweet Corn, 144
  - Zen Garden Salad with Sesame-Lime Dressing, 130–131
- Jalapeño Pizza Crunch Melt, 125–126
- Lemon Zoodles, Capers & Empress Tomatoes, 192
- Mangiameli's Family Spaghetti Sauce, 168–169
- Orlando Tomato Soup, 111–112
- Peanut & Cashew Asian Stir-Fry, 196–198
- PhoMazing Soup, 115–116
- Pulled Lion's Mane Slaw Burger, 164–167
- Spicy Chorizo Tacos, 80
- Spicy Cinnamon & Coffee Chili, 120–122
- Spicy Red Lentil Tortillas, 83

orange
- blood
  - Sparkling Blood Orange Root Beer, 56
- Fun Orange Treats, 224

orange juice
- Radicchio Rosa Salad, 141

orange liqueur
- Fit Fritz Avocado Margarita, 247

oregano
- Creature Preachers' Black Cauldron Chili, 114
- Ganis's Greek Salad, 142
- Pickled Tofu Feta, 244
- Savory Tofu Scramble on Sun-Dried Slathered Toast, 84–86
- Spicy Aztec Soup, 117–119

Orlando Tomato Soup, 111–112

P

panko
- Barbecue Italian Beyond® Loaf, 163

paprika
- Blazing Buffalo Cauliflower with Blue Cheese Crumbles, 147–148
- Creature Preachers' Black Cauldron Chili, 114
- Golden Spice Puff Pockets, 159–160
- Savory Tofu Scramble on Sun-Dried Slathered Toast, 84–86
- smoked
  - Boston Baked Lentils, 190–191
  - Easy Skillet Breakfast Potatoes, 72
  - Eggplant Bacon, 241
  - Maple-Smoked Plant Ribbons, 238
  - Spicy Cinnamon & Coffee Chili, 120–122
  - Spicy Moroccan Loaded Sweet Potato, 199
- Spicy Aztec Soup, 117–119
- Spicy Cinnamon & Coffee Chili, 120–122

Parmesan Polenta & Mushrooms, 181

parsley
- Blazing Buffalo Cauliflower with Blue Cheese Crumbles, 147–148
- Blistering Shishitos with Feta & Fiesta Smoked Crème, 92
- Chilled Tofu Mac, 137–139
- Chimichurri Chickpea & Avocado Sandwich, 149
- Mangiameli's Family Spaghetti Sauce, 168–169
- Pasta alla Bella Capri, 195
- Savory Tofu Scramble on Sun-Dried Slathered Toast, 84–86
- Spicy Chorizo Tacos, 80

pasilla pepper
- Spicy Aztec Soup, 117–119

pasta, 23
- Arugula Linguine with Lemon Zest & Capers, 193
- Cashew Crème Fraîche, 178
- Chilled Tofu Mac, 137–139
- Green Spaghetti, 175–176
- Pasta alla Bella Capri, 195

Pasta alla Bella Capri, 195

peanut butter
- Crispy Garden Rolls with Hoisin Glazed Dipping Sauce, 134–136
- Fuel Bombs, 105
- Luxurious Chocolate Masterpieces, 216–217
- Salted Caramel Fondue, 219

Peanut & Cashew Asian Stir-Fry, 196–198

peanuts
- Popcorn Paradise, 95
- Zen Garden Salad with Sesame-Lime Dressing, 130–131

Peanut Sauce, 199
- Peanut & Cashew Asian Stir-Fry, 196–198

Pear Jam, 153

pecans
- Creamy Chanterelle Soup, 109–110

peeler, 12

pepperoni, 23
- Carb-Free Pizza Bowl, 187
- Jalapeño Pizza Crunch Melt, 125–126
- Vegan Pepperoni, 250

PhoMazing Soup, 115–116

pickle chips, 23

Pickled Tofu Feta, 244
- Blistering Shishitos with Feta & Fiesta Smoked Crème, 92
- Spicy Red Lentil Tortillas, 83

pickle juice
- Chilled Tofu Mac, 137–139

Pico de Gallo, 237

Pistachio Mint Hummus, 106

pizza
- Jalapeño Pizza Crunch Melt, 125–126
- Neapolitan-Style Pizza, 248–249

pizza seasoning
- Carb-Free Pizza Bowl, 187

poblano peppers
- Green Spaghetti, 175–176

polenta
    Parmesan Polenta & Mushrooms, 181
pomegranate seeds
    Radicchio Rosa Salad, 141
Popcorn Paradise, 95
potatoes
    Creature Preachers' Black Cauldron Chili, 114
    Easy Skillet Breakfast Potatoes, 72
    Garlic Mashed Potatoes & Sweet Corn, 144
    red
        Golden Spice Puff Pockets, 159–160
    sweet
        Creature Preachers' Black Cauldron Chili, 114
        Orlando Tomato Soup, 111–112
        Spicy Moroccan Loaded Sweet Potato, 199
prebiotics, 29
probiotics, 29
Prosecco Pickled Jalapeños, 242
    Spicy Chorizo Tacos, 80
protein powder
    raspberry
        Raspberry & Cardamom Smoothie, 60
Pulled Lion's Mane Slaw Burger, 164–167
pumpkin seeds
    Cashew Basil Blitz, 173–174

R

Radicchio Rosa Salad, 141
ramekins, 12
ramen, 24
Raspberry & Cardamom Smoothie, 60
Ratatouille, 177
red pepper flakes
    Easy Skillet Breakfast Potatoes, 72
Reishi Mushroom Turmeric Latte, 226
rice paper
    Maple-Smoked Plant Ribbons, 238
rice syrup, 259
Roasted Eggplant Tzatziki, 188
Roasted Rosemary Naked Almonds, 96
Rocky Road Fudge, 209
rosemary
    Cashew Crème Fraîche, 178
    Chilled Tofu Mac, 137–139
    Roasted Rosemary Naked Almonds, 96
    Sparkling Chocolate Blueberries & Mint Elixir, 55
Rose Petal Elixir, 47
Rustic Cornbread Skillet, 185–186

S

salad
    Ganis's Greek Salad, 142
    Radicchio Rosa Salad, 141
    Spicy Mango Salad, 133
    Zen Garden Salad with Sesame-Lime Dressing, 130–131
salt
    Himalayan
        Sole, 48
Salted Caramel Fondue, 219
sandwich
    Chimichurri Chickpea & Avocado Sandwich, 149
    Savory Tofu Scramble on Sun-Dried Slathered Toast, 84–86
seasoning
    pizza, 24
sesame seeds
    Crispy Garden Rolls with Hoisin Glazed Dipping Sauce, 134–136
shallot
    No-Crab Crab Cakes, 94
    Ratatouille, 177
shishito peppers
    Blistering Shishitos with Feta & Fiesta Smoked Crème, 92
SIBO, 27–28
smoothie
    Electrolyte Tropical Smoothie, 63
    Raspberry & Cardamom Smoothie, 60
Sole, 48
Electrolyte Fruit Punch, 49
sopes
    Abuela's Fried Sopes, 157–158
sorbet
    Cherry Sorbet, 213
sorbitol, 28
soup
    Creamy Chanterelle Soup, 109–110
    Creature Preachers' Black Cauldron Chili, 114
    Orlando Tomato Soup, 111–112
    PhoMazing Soup, 115–116
    Spicy Aztec Soup, 117–119
sour cream, 24
sourdough discard
    Crispy Sourdough Bread Sticks, 150
sourdough starter, 152
soyrizo
    Spicy Chorizo Tacos, 80
Sparkling Blood Orange Root Beer, 56
Sparkling Chocolate Blueberries & Mint Elixir, 55
Spicy Aztec Soup, 117–119
Spicy Chorizo Tacos, 80
Spicy Cinnamon & Coffee Chili, 120–122
Spicy Garlic Aioli, 234
Spicy Mango Salad, 133
Spicy Moroccan Loaded Sweet Potato, 199
Spicy Red Lentil Tortillas, 83
spinach
    Carb-Free Pizza Bowl, 187

Cashew Basil Blitz, 173–174
Peanut & Cashew Asian Stir-Fry, 196–198
Savory Tofu Scramble on Sun-Dried Slathered Toast, 84–86
Spicy Chorizo Tacos, 80
Spicy Moroccan Loaded Sweet Potato, 199
spring roll wrappers
    Crispy Garden Rolls with Hoisin Glazed Dipping Sauce, 134–136
squash
    yellow
        Ratatouille, 177
        Sun-Kissed Capers & Squash, 87
sriracha
    Crispy Garden Rolls with Hoisin Glazed Dipping Sauce, 134–136
    Peanut Sauce, 199
    Spicy Red Lentil Tortillas, 83
    Zen Garden Salad with Sesame-Lime Dressing, 130–131
star anise
    Reishi Mushroom Turmeric Latte, 226
stir-fry
    Peanut & Cashew Asian Stir-Fry, 196–198
strawberries
    Messy Loaded Almond Yogurt & Banana Nut Crunch, 73
Strawberry Fields Forever Donuts, 256–258
sucrose, 260
sugar, 31–33, 259–263
sugar alcohols, 28
sunflower seeds
    Aloha Kakahiaka Overnight Oats, 79
    Roasted Eggplant Tzatziki, 188
Sun-Kissed Capers & Squash, 87

T

tacos
    Spicy Chorizo Tacos, 80
tahini
    Pistachio Mint Hummus, 106
tamari
    Crispy Garden Rolls with Hoisin Glazed Dipping Sauce, 134–136
    Eggplant Bacon, 241
    Maple-Smoked Plant Ribbons, 238
    Peanut & Cashew Asian Stir-Fry, 196–198
    Peanut Sauce, 199
    PhoMazing Soup, 115–116
    Spicy Moroccan Loaded Sweet Potato, 199
    Vegan Pepperoni, 250
    Zen Garden Salad with Sesame-Lime Dressing, 130–131
tapioca flour
    Cali Almond Flour Crackers, 101–102

Index   281

tea
    Chamomile & Pink Lemonade Kombucha Fizz, 51
    green
        Lemon Drop Healing Tonic, 65
tequila
    Fit Fritz Avocado Margarita, 247
thermometer, 12
thyme
    Barbecue Italian Beyond® Loaf, 163
    Cashew Crème Fraîche, 178
    Chilled Tofu Mac, 137–139
    Creamy Caprese Seduction, 127–128
    Creamy Chanterelle Soup, 109–110
    Parmesan Polenta & Mushrooms, 181
    Pickled Tofu Feta, 244
    Ratatouille, 177
    Savory Tofu Scramble on Sun-Dried Slathered Toast, 84–86
Tiki Love Potion, 52
toaster oven, 13
tofu
    Chilled Tofu Mac, 137–139
    Peanut & Cashew Asian Stir-Fry, 196–198
    Pickled Tofu Feta, 244
    Savory Tofu Scramble on Sun-Dried Slathered Toast, 84–86
tomatoes
    cherry
        Chilled Tofu Mac, 137–139
        Savory Tofu Scramble on Sun-Dried Slathered Toast, 84–86
    Creamy Caprese Seduction, 127–128
    crushed
        Mangiameli's Family Spaghetti Sauce, 168–169
        Pasta alla Bella Capri, 195
    fire-roasted
        Bold Border Sauce, 182
        Carb-Free Pizza Bowl, 187
        Creature Preachers' Black Cauldron Chili, 114
        Spicy Aztec Soup, 117–119
    Ganis's Greek Salad, 142
    grape
        Arugula Linguine with Lemon Zest & Capers, 193
        Creamy Caprese Seduction, 127–128
    Jalapeño Pizza Crunch Melt, 125–126
    Orlando Tomato Soup, 111–112
    Pico de Gallo, 237
    purreed
        Spicy Cinnamon & Coffee Chili, 120–122
    Ratatouille, 177
    sun-dried, 24
        Fire-Kissed Gouda Bites, 100

Lemon Zoodles, Capers & Empress Tomatoes, 192
    Sun-Kissed Capers & Squash, 87
tomato paste
    Barbecue Italian Beyond® Loaf, 163
    Mangiameli's Family Spaghetti Sauce, 168–169
    sun-dried, 24–25
        Jalapeño Pizza Crunch Melt, 125–126
        Savory Tofu Scramble on Sun-Dried Slathered Toast, 84–86
tomato sauce, 25
    Mangiameli's Family Spaghetti Sauce, 168–169
tortillas
    Boston Baked Lentils, 190–191
    Easy Flour Tortillas, 253
    Golden Spice Puff Pockets, 159–160
    Roasted Eggplant Tzatziki, 188
    Spicy Chorizo Tacos, 80
    Spicy Red Lentil Tortillas, 83
Truffle Joy Bombs, 214
turmeric, 41
    Golden Spice Puff Pockets, 159–160
    Lemon Drop Healing Tonic, 65
    Reishi Mushroom Turmeric Latte, 226
    Savory Tofu Scramble on Sun-Dried Slathered Toast, 84–86
Turmeric Golden Paste, 42–44
    Golden Milk, 225
24-Carrot Gold, 91
tzatziki
    Roasted Eggplant Tzatziki, 188
tzatziki seasoning
    Spicy Garlic Aioli, 234

U

udon noodles
    Peanut & Cashew Asian Stir-Fry, 196–198
Ultimate Tsunami Cacao, 226

V

vanilla extract
    Chaga Frappé, 66
    Edible Maple Almond Chocolate Chip Oat Cookie Dough, 205
    Luxurious Chocolate Masterpieces, 216–217
    Maple Almond Chocolate Chip Overnight Oats, 76
    Rocky Road Fudge, 209
    Salted Caramel Fondue, 219
    Strawberry Fields Forever Donuts, 256–258
    Truffle Joy Bombs, 214
    Ultimate Tsunami Cacao, 226
Vegan Pepperoni, 250
vegetables, 27

vinegar
    apple cider
        Boston Baked Lentils, 190–191
        Cashew Crèma Mexicana, 232
        Fire & Flux, 59
        Pulled Lion's Mane Slaw Burger, 164–167
        Spicy Garlic Aioli, 234
        Strawberry Fields Forever Donuts, 256–258
        White Cheddar & Broccoli, 145
    champagne
        Radicchio Rosa Salad, 141
    coconut
        Spicy Garlic Aioli, 234
    prosecco wine
        Prosecco Pickled Jalapeños, 242
    red wine
        Ganis's Greek Salad, 142
    white
        Peanut Sauce, 199
        Pickled Tofu Feta, 244
    white balsamic
        Bold Border Sauce, 182
        Chilled Tofu Mac, 137–139
        Crispy Garden Rolls with Hoisin Glazed Dipping Sauce, 134–136
        White Cheddar & Broccoli, 145
        Zen Garden Salad with Sesame-Lime Dressing, 130–131

W

White Cheddar & Broccoli, 145
Worcestershire sauce
    Eggplant Bacon, 241

X

xylitol, 28

Y

yogurt
    Berry Chia Dream, 74
    vanilla
        Maple Almond Chocolate Chip Oat Cookie Dough Pops, 206
    vanilla almond
        Messy Loaded Almond Yogurt & Banana Nut Crunch, 73
Yuka (app), 15

Z

Zen Garden Salad with Sesame-Lime Dressing, 130–131
zucchini
    Lemon Zoodles, Capers & Empress Tomatoes, 192
    Ratatouille, 177